A GIFT FOR:

_____

FROM:

_____

To fuel your success

ON

_____

RECORDING MY TREE TALKS

WHEN TREES TALK

31 Mind-Shifting Tree Talks with Life Lessons in Personal Development and Success

Extra MILE Innovators
Kingston, Jamaica W.I.

Published by
Extra MILE Innovators
Kingston, Jamaica

Editing by
Tamara Francis

Cover Art by
Nadine Jardine

Illustrations by
Lika Kvirikashvili

Print & eBook Layout by
N.D. Author Services [NDAS]
www.NDAuthorServices.com

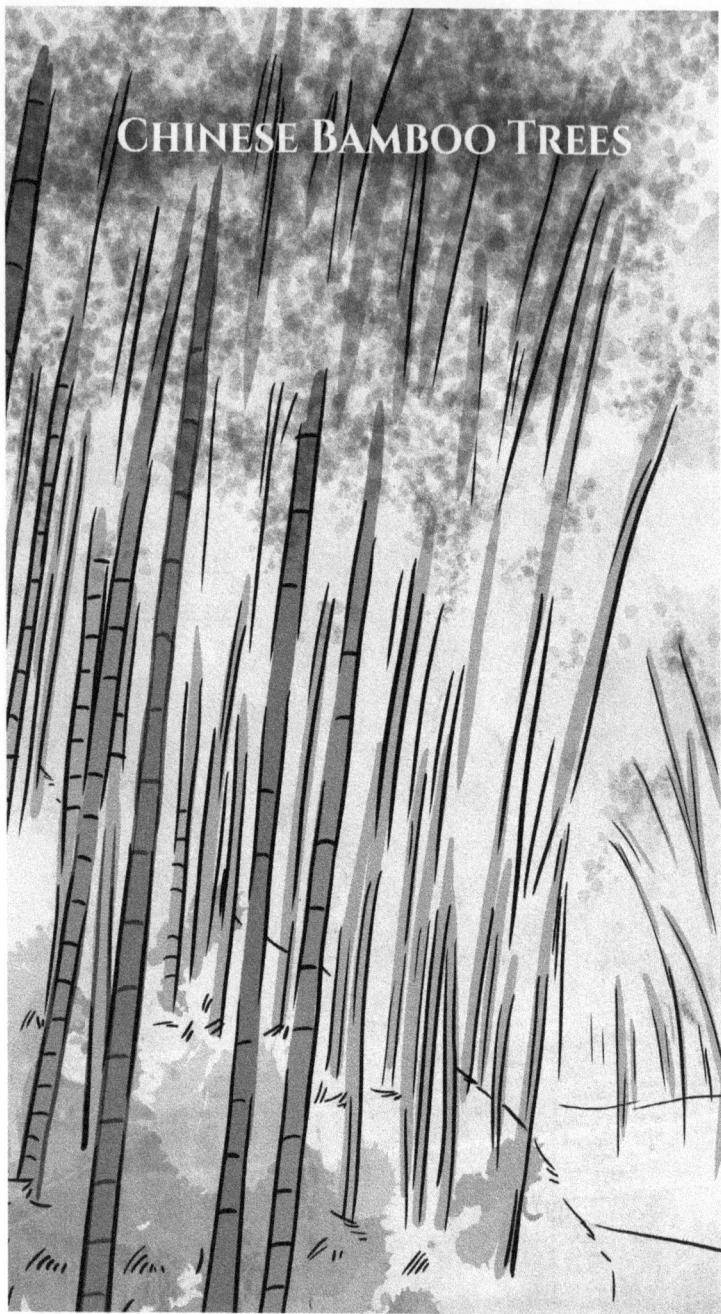

CHINESE BAMBOO TREES

NOTES

Scripture verses are quoted from The New Century Version and The New King James Version of the Holy Bible.

For permission requests, write to the publisher at the address below.

Extra MILE Innovators
21 Phoenix Avenue
Kingston 10, Jamaica W.I.
Telephone: (1876) 782-9893
www.extramileja.com
extramileinnovators@gmail.com

ABOUT THE AUTHOR

Cameka "Ruth" Taylor is an educator, speaker and personal development coach. She is a Christian who is passionate about people maximizing their potential and living the meaningful, productive and successful life they were designed to live. Arising from her experiences of overcoming years of heartache and pain, Cameka founded Extra MILE Innovators, a personal development company dedicated to spreading hope and teaching people how to rise above adversity to achieve success. Through Extra MILE Innovators, she creates diverse tools, initiatives and programmes to motivate, inspire, liberate and empower others to achieve their life goals.

Cameka is a former registrar of the Jamaica Theological Seminary as well as an adjunct lecturer. She served as a missionary with Operation Mobilization and has been personally involved in cross-cultural Christian missions since 2003, ministering in countries in the Caribbean, Latin America, Africa and Europe. Additionally, she mentors girls from inner city communities and speaks regularly in churches and schools across Jamaica. With the recent creation of her Design to Win and Behind TheSmile initiatives Cameka's mission to spread hope and empower people has been further strengthened.

Cameka holds an M.A. in Theology from the Caribbean Graduate School of Theology; a B.A in General Studies from the Jamaica Theological Seminary and a Diploma in Teaching from Mico Teachers' College. She resides in Kingston, Jamaica.

To mom,
Whom I have grown to greatly
admire and whose footsteps in
personal growth, financial
wisdom and success, I now seek
to emulate.

PRAISE FOR THE BOOK

It is truly a gift to be able to listen to trees - an exceptional gift that Cameka Taylor is not ashamed of. Her passion to impact lives has allowed you and me to reap the fruit borne from her gift: this book filled with 31 mind-shifting Tree Talks and 100 life-giving lessons in personal development. I'm one of the most privileged people alive because of my relationship with Cameka. With almost 2 decades of memories between us, I've had the opportunity to see firsthand how one can trod from a path of heartache and bondage to a highway of contagious joy and emancipation while churning out success after success. This book is not just a collection of 'nice ideas' but a toolkit filled with seeds, that when sown and nurtured in your mind, will bloom and bear the significant, satisfying and vibrant life you are meant to live. *When Trees Talk* will soon become your favourite resource for designing the life you love. The trees around do talk; and with this book, you can start listening today.

—*Didan Ashanta*
Author & LifeDesigner, Japan

Cameka shares fresh revelations on achieving success. Whatever your definition of success is, we all struggle with the desire to free ourselves from the restraints that hold us back from it, but sometimes don't know exactly how to. In an engaging, natural and highly creative way, Cameka carries on a conversation not only with trees but with the reader. It is a conversation that will help revolutionise how you see your life now and unlock the potential in you that is waiting to be realized. This book challenges you to see success as a journey—it is something you achieve moment by moment as you stay the course.

I would strongly encourage anyone to get this book!

—Sharma L. Taylor, Ph.D
Attorney-at-Law

Following the success of her first book, a raw, authentic and heartfelt biography of a life captured by the grace of God, Cameka "Ruth" Taylor scores another hit in her new book, *"When Trees Talk,"* a series of insightful and helpful tools that propel personal development. Whether you are a professional or student or desiring only to be more effective in life, this book is for you. It will give you the tools you need for a successful and meaningful life.

This is the type of book that you keep for a lifetime, because the lessons you will find in it are life principles that span generations and seasons of life.

Want to get the best out of this book? Read it slowly, make notes, apply liberally.

—Kenyatta E. Lewis
Field Director HBF, Vision Caribbean

As a dreamer of great dreams, I somewhat felt as though I were eating while taking in these sumptuous revelations. This isn't just a book but a manual and companion in one. It instructs yet guides and walks with you. From the heart of the author, we are inspired to learn, grow and change as she candidly shares glimpses of her life journey. The book is informative, yet compelling; a dash of intrigue and you are tempted to read ahead. There are no age limits here as the balance is struck between believing God and allowing Him to work out that belief tangibly through our lives.

I have encountered this material at a crucial point in my own journey and am able to say the wisdom of the trees will ignite a desire in you to pursue God and His purposes for your life.

—Chosen Jenny
Disciple

The book *When Trees Talk* can be used as an interactive devotional guide for all Christians. The key principles from this book have been chosen for the readers to re-examine their life in different situations. Each day, there are soul-searching questions along with quotes and scriptural references to help persons understand their purpose. It is with an awesome sense of responsibility and obedience that the author committed herself to the task of writing and sharing with us out of experience what God has given to her. The author knows the value of intimacy with God and invites her readers to the same. I would recommend this book to small groups as well as individuals who would love to walk in their purpose.

—Dr. Shonna Ann Leigh
Acting Principal/Academic Dean
Midland Bible Institute

CONTENTS

FOREWORD

Collective human experience confirms the value and importance of trees. They are absolutely essential and vital to the health, well-being, viability, and sustainability of human society. Trees provide food, oxygen, shelter, economic opportunity; contribute to water conservation, soil preservation, enable protection for wildlife, air filtration, and support healthy climates. Trees also facilitate opportunities for rest and relaxation, meditation and solitude, and in many instances persons have special memories associated with events and activities related to trees. Trees are essential to life.

We enjoy and benefit from trees, even if we seldom demonstrate our appreciation of their value. But, who knew that they talked?

The book *When Trees Talk* supports the truth that trees are valuable. It provides an additional avenue through which to appreciate their contribution to enhancing human experience. They talk! And, wow, do they talk in Cameka's book. They talk about success, overcoming adversities, values, personal transformation, achieving goals, and appreciating opportunities around us, planning, valuing and releasing the star in each one of us; being fruitful. Their collective message provides a base for effective living. Cameka skilfully orchestrates the lessons to the benefit of all readers.

Cameka Taylor is special. She is one of those rare individuals who ooze integrity, sincerity, charisma and thus, believability. She writes with passion and a freedom that is refreshing. She does not care if you think that she may be emotionally challenged or delusional. She converses with trees. She is free. She has encountered the liberation that comes from fully appreciating the natural environment and its storehouse of treasures, as liberally provided by our Creator—God!

Cameka writes as someone who has lived the lessons she is teaching and passing on to others through the pages of her enlightening book. She knows firsthand the critical lessons learnt from living her purpose, and actively facing the challenges life presents to each one of us. Thankfully, she is not selfish. These lessons and how we might benefit from them are shared for our benefit.

We all have goals and desires relative to personal development. We sometimes refer to the outcomes of this process as SUCCESS. Some call it PROSPERITY. Others use the word ABUNDANCE. Persons will use different words to describe the positive outcomes desired. Whatever word(s) we use, we face the challenge of short-termism, whereby we want instant success, etc. We seldom fail to appreciate the fact that all of life, and all segments or phases of it, is a journey. A journey that, yes, will at times realise fairly quickly outcomes; but also, like the bamboo tree, outcomes that take an inordinately long period to even show signs of life, let alone growth, and then all of a sudden will burst into a process of rapid growth. This is the stuff of which life is made. Frustrating yet intriguing; depressing and exhilarating; painful but worth every minute. Life, well worth the living! Enjoy *When Trees Talk*. Start your process of enjoying, growing and nurturing the life you have today.

—Dameon A. Black
    Higher Education Professional qualified in
        Theology, Education and Management

PREFACE

It was a day that turned my life around and the day I learnt a valuable lesson from a tree. **"What's worth having is worth waiting for."** On that fateful day, my eyes swelled with tears when I came off the phone after talking with a friend. The reality of my poor financial health was staring me coldly in the face and I felt terrible! I had at that time an urgent personal need to take care of and my friend was offering me services free of charge to meet the need, but I could not take up the offer because I simply could not afford the small transportation cost to get to the venue. I remember how my voice trembled on the phone as I tried to maintain my composure and fight back the tears. I remember the feeling of shame and embarrassment that I felt when I had to tell my friend the truth about my finances that day!

Moreover, the sting of pain only increased as I questioned myself. *Should I really have turned down those teaching offers to pursue a dream of starting my own personal development company to write and speak for transformation? Why am I prolonging my financial struggle like one who has had no education and training? Is this dream worth pursuing?* And yet, in those moments of frustration as I questioned my newfound mission, I knew deep down that this, too, would pass, and that one day I would look back and laugh in triumph over this moment. I knew all too well from experience that, despite being unable to meet the immediate need, help was probably on the way but at that moment I was broken.

Yet in the midst of my brokenness, I kept remembering lessons from my personal development training and I knew I needed to fight the negative feelings. I decided to fight the feelings with gratitude and find the seed of equivalent benefit in my situation, and by that I mean, find a lesson in my situation or imagine how this could be used for good in the end. Thus, as the tears flowed, I started singing the song, "I've got a roof up above me, a place to sleep, food on my table and shoes on my feet. You gave me your love, Lord, and a fine family, so I thank you, Lord, for your blessings on me." Moments later, I turned to my own blog for encouragement and found one of my blog posts about lessons on the success journey from the Chinese bamboo tree. It was then that the Chinese bamboo tree spoke to me and reminded me of a vital life lesson: **"What's worth having is worth waiting for. You are making a difference. Stay on the path. Your change will come. Don't give up!"**

That conversation with the Chinese bamboo tree renewed my vision and comforted me and the very next day a friend visited me unannounced and encouraged me to stay the course. He then took me to get the service I needed and gave me some financial assistance. Before the day ended, I again received more financial help from another source. What's more, a few days later, I received an unexpected sum of money from another friend who was visiting from overseas. That friend also treated me to dinner in a fine Chinese restaurant. Yes, dinner at a Chinese restaurant! The irony was not lost on me.

The Chinese bamboo tree is the symbol of my personal development company, Extra MILE Innovators and of all the tree talks and stories over the years, the Chinese bamboo tree has been my greatest inspiration in the achievement of my goals.

Like the Chinese bamboo tree, which takes years to develop below the ground and then grows 90 feet tall, at an unbelievable rate, I too, must patiently develop this new phase of my journey, with the expectation that, in time, I will grow 90 feet tall.

When the days prove difficult and the tears flow, the tree lessons I blog about give me hope and courage. I also realize that these blogs are not just helping me. The feedback I receive on social media shows that these tree talks are encouraging others along their journey. It is these blogs that have now been transformed into a book of inspiration to fuel your success. This is in direct response to an article which a friend on Facebook sent me about blogging a book.

Now you have in your hand, this inspirational book: ***WHEN TREES TALK: 31 Mind-Shifting Tree Talks with Life Lessons in Personal Development and Success.*** When Trees Talk is meant to be used over the course of 31 days as your daily dose of encouragement and inspiration. Each tree talk has three lessons to *motivate* you to achieve your goals. At the end of the book, there is also a bonus talk: *7 Life Changing Habits to Fuel Your Success,* making a grand total of 100 life lessons for your personal development and success.

When Trees Talk is for those who are in search of purpose, and for those in pursuit of their goals and dreams who are feeling frustrated, and need encouragement to stay the course. It is ideal for the young who are facing a crisis of identity versus role confusion and for those who are seeking to make something meaningful of their lives. It is even more ideal for those who have made mistakes and by virtue of adversity, like my mom, have given up on their dreams, and need a word of inspiration, courage and reasons to try again, so that like her, they can pick themselves up and go on to achieve something more. Whether you are a struggling student, parent, employee, entrepreneur or just someone striving for success, these tree talks will show you how to get to the next level. It's time to hear and heed the wisdom of the trees. Join me now as we learn to talk, grow and live successfully like trees.

—Cameka "Ruth" Taylor, April 2016

HOW TO USE THIS BOOK

Welcome to an exciting 31 day journey of personal development, inspiration and enlightenment which will propel you farther along your journey to success! If you are striving for success or trying to figure out what to do with your life or have taken the leap to pursue your dreams, pay careful attention to the guidelines and recommended uses which are given in this section.

Here are some guidelines as you take this journey:

1. Set aside time daily to read each talk.
2. Reflect on the three lessons in each talk.
3. Write a response or course of action that you will take as a result of the lessons shared in each talk.
4. Share the lessons you learn with others.
5. Choose five habits that you will adopt which will lead to your success.
6. Write a review of the book and post it on Amazon, Goodreads or on the author's Facebook page.

RECOMMENDED USES

This book is a tool which can be used in a variety of contexts. Here are some platforms or media for using this book:

1. Seminars, conferences and workshops on Personal Development

2. Courses in Career Development
3. Life skills coaching programmes
4. Human Resource and Staff Development
5. Guidance and Counselling programmes
6. Empowerment groups and Non-profit organizations
7. Bedside readings, coffee table readings
8. Personal use for self development, inspiration and motivation
9. Church and Church related ministries for all teens and adults
10. Primary schools, high schools and tertiary institutions
11. Small group or large group book study sessions
12. Content for motivational speeches/talks
13. Give it away as gifts to fuel the success of another

Enjoy your reading of *When Trees Talk. Go forth and **BECOME** all you were designed to be!*

INTRODUCTION

"Don't you sleep at nights?"asked Von, quite astute in her observation. I explained, in answer to her question, that I was working on my new book, and she nodded with understanding. Lately, I felt like an insomniac as the trees constantly flooded my mind with nuggets of wisdom and like a professional scribe I just could not stop writing. It was 2 a.m. and all I could do was: write! It sounds crazy but yes, the trees were talking and I felt compelled to record the revelations of wisdom. I then wrote with a passion and intensity reminiscent of the penning of my first book and I knew instinctively that this would be my second published work. Who knew that trees could create such passion and intensity and wonderful inspiration?

Nevertheless, this early morning session was merely an appetizer. As the day wore on there would be more revelations. It was Saturday which meant doing the usual domestic chores including raking the yard and cleaning the house. I often don't mind raking the yard because this activity usually gives me time to think, but I never imagined on this occasion, how delightfully impactful it would be. That morning, I took note for the first time, of all the trees in my backyard. There were seven different trees and six were fruit trees: mango, banana, soursop, lime, moringa, pear (avocado) and palm. In close proximity were my neighbour's breadfruit, mango and ackee trees whose branches and limps had decided to trespass on our property. As I raked the yard, the trees in the backyard began to speak to me once again. They became the sage on a stage and I was an attentive student in the lecture theatre of my backyard.

I, therefore, paused my raking, went for a pen and paper and began furiously taking notes. With fascination, I noticed for the first time that the mango, pear, soursop, lime and breadfruit trees all had fruits. Some were ready to be harvested and eaten while others were at different stages of their development. The pear tree was still at the stage of having many young undeveloped fruit and the mangoes were mature and at the stage of dropping to the ground much to my daily delight. My observations continued when suddenly, the trees turned the spotlight on me. They began making my life part of their discourse, challenging me about my habits, attitudes and philosophy of living and giving me important instructions regarding my future. In that moment, I felt challenged and commissioned. I felt the trees were giving me insights to share with the world and commissioning me to become a tree ambassador, to share their golden nuggets of wisdom with the world. I giggled at the thought and mused about becoming known as the "Tree Lady" and saw flashes of myself giving motivational talks and other presentations on life lessons from trees for personal growth and success.

It is these insights and revelations which have redefined my outlook on life and my plans for the future. I believe they will redefine your outlook on life and challenge you to develop the philosophy, attitudes and habits which will lead to your personal success. I am confident that these tree talks will move you one step closer to realizing your dream of achieving success. Get ready for transformation! It's time to **talk, grow and live successfully like trees!** He who has an ear to hear let him hear and heed the wisdom of the trees!

PART I:
TALK LIKE TREES

If you would know strength and patience,
welcome the company of trees.
—Hal Borland

Recording My Tree Talks

TALK 1
THE CHINESE BAMBOO TREE:
THE JOURNEY TO SUCCESS

Success is not final. Failure is not fatal:
It is the courage to continue that counts.
—Winston Churchill

YOUR VISION IS POSSIBLE

IT'S POSSIBLE. Those were the two words that changed my life dramatically in September 2010. I was engaged to be married for the first time and yet I was quite unhappy. Then one night as I browsed You-Tube, I heard a motivational message by the highly acclaimed author and speaker, Les Brown, in which he spoke those two life changing words: it's possible. In that speech Les introduced to me the story of the Chinese Bamboo tree. By now many persons are familiar with the story but it was the first time I was hearing it and I have never forgotten it. In fact, the Chinese bamboo tree is now part of my company logo. Les explained to his audience some of the challenges that we often face when chasing our dreams or striving for success and he used the Chinese bamboo tree to offer hope and insights to overcome the challenges and achieve success. Today, I'll repeat the story of the Chinese bamboo tree and eke out three lessons about the journey to success.

In the Far East, said Les, there is a particular Chinese Bamboo tree planted as a seed which needs to be watered daily for five years before it emerges from the soil. The owner daily waters and fertilizes the ground where the seed has been planted, although year after year nothing happens. Then an amazing thing happens in the fifth year! In six weeks, it grows 90 feet tall! Les then asked the question: Did it grow 90 feet tall in six weeks or five years? The answer is obvious. It took five years. If at any point the owner had given up there would be no tree. Les in his inimitable style jokes: "Imagine you tell your neighbours you are growing a Chinese bamboo tree and year after year nothing emerges. One comes and says: 'I hear you are growing a Chinese bamboo tree but even Stevie Wonder and Ray Charles [two blind artistes] can see that nothing is happening.' Sadly, people will mock you when your dream takes a while to fulfill but you must never give up the dream. So what three lessons can we learn from the Chinese bamboo tree?

LESSON 1: SUCCESS IS A JOURNEY; IT DOES NOT HAPPEN OVERNIGHT

This first lesson from the Chinese bamboo tree is obvious. It's a journey. Therefore, keep watering and believing in your dream or that goal that you have; once you see it, firmly believe it and keep working at it. *You have to believe in your dream even when others can't see it and persevere.* "Success," explains Earl Nightingale, "is the progressive realization of a worthy goal or ideal." It is important to note here that the mark of true success goes beyond financial prosperity. It is fulfilling your purpose and doing well that which you were designed do while on this earth and making sure you are at peace with God, your Divine Designer.

LESSON 2: DON'T LOSE SIGHT OF THE VISION ON THE JOURNEY TO SUCCESS

This second lesson reminds me of a bible verse, Habakkuk 2: 2-3: "Write the vision. Make it clear on tablets so that anyone can read it quickly. This vision is for a future time. It describes the end, and it will be fulfilled. If it seems slow in coming, wait patiently, for it will surely take place. It will not be delayed." Everything has a season. If at any time the grower had lost sight of the end and stopped watering the tree, it (the dream) would have been aborted. Success experts like Brian Tracy often tell us to daily: re-write our goals or to look at them twice daily when you rise and before going to bed. It's important to keep it before you because as Rohn says, "Everything by longevity tends to go off track." Stay on course, my friend. Don't lose sight of your vision.

LESSON 3: BECOME ALL YOU CAN BE ON THE JOURNEY TO SUCCESS

In the fifth year, in 6 weeks, the bamboo tree grows 90 feet tall. It does not just emerge from the soil. It maximizes its potential. I once heard a lecture where Jim Rohn stated, "Trees don't grow half. A tree grows to its full height. Humans are the only ones that don't maximize their potential." Be like the Chinese Bamboo tree! Grow 90 feet tall! Rohn further encouraged: "Become all you can be on the road to success. Don't settle for mediocrity." Therefore, work on all the skills you can. Give all you can. Help all you can. Learn all you can on the journey to success. Maximize your potential and become outstanding. A key way to do this is through continual practice and honing of your skill. Malcolm Gladwell, in *Outliers*, speaks about the 10,000 hour rule. Those who achieve mastery in a field and stand out are those who practice in the area for at least 10,000 hours. When you are passionate about something, those 10,000 hours will go by quickly. If you pursue your passion 40 hours a week, practise that skill or utilize that gift for 40 hours each week. Within 5-7 years, you will become outstanding and stand out in your field. And guess what? The rewards of success will be yours. This journey of becoming all we can to achieve success is what I call **personal development**. Start that journey today or stay on the course.

WHAT IS THE CHINESE BAMBOO TREE SAYING TO YOU?

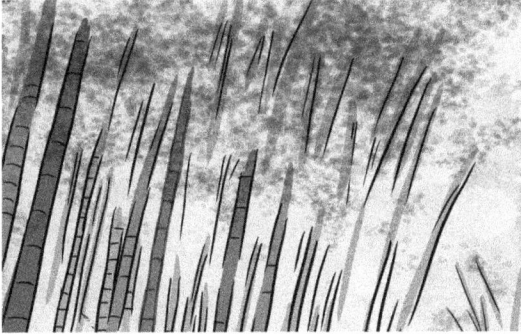

Am I the only one to whom the Chinese bamboo tree is speaking? What is it saying to you? What's your vision? To what journey are you called? Are you seeing it clearly? Do you still believe in it, despite the criticisms? Have you given up nourishing your vision because others are laughing at or mocking you? Go forth and become all you can be on the road to success. Don't settle for mediocrity. Work on all the skills you can. Invest in your personal development. Don't lose sight of the vision and remember it will not happen overnight. I hope these three lessons will inspire you on your success journey.

Where there is a will, you will definitely find a way. Stay tuned for tomorrow's tree talk with the olive tree on overcoming adversities.

RESPONSE TO TREE TALK

What actions will you take as a result of this tree talk? Or what decisions will you make?

TALK 2
THE OLIVE TREE:
OVERCOMING ADVERSITIES

*The size of your success is measured
by the strength of your desire; the size of
your dream; and how you handle
disappointment along the way.
—Robert Kiyosaki*

PLANET ADVERSITY

Adversity is not some special gift reserved for the poor. I've coined this phrase as an adaptation to something Jim Rohn once said in a personal development presentation: *"Disappointment is not some special gift reserved for the poor."* You will see that I make mention of Rohn repeatedly. In 2010, Rohn became my foremost E-tutor on personal development and success through his audio books and presentations. Whether you are rich or poor, you will face disappointment and adversity. Two of the more painful ones include divorce and death. Abandonment, rejection, betrayal, unmet desires, emotional, physical or sexual abuse, sickness, you name it, will come our way because that's just the way things are on this planet. Nevertheless, while we have no control over the adversities we face on this planet, we have control over this one thing: **Our response to adversity.** Today, I'd like to eke out three lessons on facing adversity from the olive tree and how we can respond well to adversity.

For many thousands of years the olive was the basis of life in the Mediterranean world. Olive trees still grow richly today. Even in dry, arid areas, the olive tree is helped to grow by placing "rock mulching" around its base to precipitate (to force the making of more) dew. The olive tree can survive all manner of damage. Burned, it sprouts again. Cut down, there is always hope that the tree will send up a new shoot, even appearing to have been dead for years. Like humans, it takes the olive tree 17 to 30 years to reach its full vintage, and its best fruit is in riper years. It lives for centuries. The olive tree has many uses. The fruit is used for eating, its oil for cooking and for lighting lamps. The wood is richly grained and sturdy. After the great flood, it was a freshly sprouted olive leaf that the dove brought to Noah. Throughout the ages the olive has stood for peace, for steadfast love, for undeserved favour (mercy) and newness of life.

LESSON 4: YOU CAN FLOURISH DESPITE THE ADVERSITY BEING EXPERIENCED

Although we, too, live in a world of hardship, adversity and disappointment, let us find a way to flourish like the green olive tree. The olive tree has become the enduring symbol of the attitude I should have in life. The olive tree is not like the banana tree which is so common in the parish of my birth: St Mary. The banana tree cannot withstand a strong wind. It is easily blown down in the face of strong assault. We cannot afford to be like the banana tree but, rather, like the olive tree. It survived the flood in Noah's time. It thrived even with so much water on the land for 150 days, which should have rotted its roots. It stood up to the assaults. The best way I know how to thrive in the face of adversity is through Divine aid. Psalm 46 is one of my favourite passages: "God is our refuge and strength, a very present help in trouble." Let's seek Divine aid and be determined to flourish amidst adversities. "We shall overcome!" should be your mantra. It may take a while to bounce back, but bounce back! Don't lose hope whatever the adversity!

LESSON 5: YOU CAN BECOME A SYMBOL OF NEWNESS OF LIFE IN SPITE OF ADVERSITY

Throughout the ages the olive has stood for peace, for steadfast love, for undeserved favour (mercy) and newness of life. Napoleon Hill said: "There is a seed of equivalent benefit in every adversity." Romans 8: 28 says God works in all things for the good of those who love him and are called according to his purpose. When you are in pain, I'm sure it's hard to see how any good can come out of your adversity but if you learn **to train yourself** to find the good, or the opportunity in every bad situation, small or great, you will find it. And then little by little you will become stronger and filled with hope. Others looking on will be intrigued. You will become a 'glass half full' person and eventually a symbol of hope. Don't dwell indefinitely on the wrong done to you or the regrets of the past. Fight discouragement. Find a way to turn your lemon into lemonade, your handicap into a symbol of strength. For example, some who've lost loved ones to cancer, now spend their time and effort finding a cure for cancer or support-ing those affected by cancer. The girl once raped now helps with legislation to protect victims of rape and educates others on how to not let rape destroy their lives. Former battered women now become act-ivists and open shelters for battered women. The examples are all around us. There are many models to emulate.

LESSON 6: YOU CAN OVERCOME YOUR ADVERSITY AND LEAVE A LASTING LEGACY

Unlike human beings, olive trees live for centuries and many generations of humans benefit from these olive trees. A tree that lives for centuries has cer-tainly weathered many storms. The olive tree does this excellently and is an evergreen tree. It adjusts well to the storms of life. Although we may not live for centuries our response to adversity can leave an inerasable mark that will be remembered for centur-ies. Today, we speak of Jesus of Nazareth who died several centuries ago. He triumphed over great adversities. His disciples wrote of his tales in books which we now read to inspire us. The names of Mar-cus Garvey, Martin Luther King, Nelson Mandela and biblical characters like King David, Queen Esther, Joseph and Ruth all still live on because they allowed their adversity to make them better not bitter.

Responding positively to adversity can cause your name to be remembered for centuries, long after you die. Quitters will be forgotten but those who conquer and rise above their adversity to make a difference will be long remembered. Let's study how great men and women overcame their adversit-ies and set out to leave a lasting legacy for centuries so that like the olive tree our name and story will live on for centuries.

WHAT IS THE OLIVE TREE SAYING TO YOU?

Will you be an olive tree or a banana tree? Determine to flourish, to arise from your adversity and find newness of life. Determine despite your adversity that you will leave a lasting legacy for generations to come!

Where there is a will, you will definitely find a way. Stay tuned for tomorrow's tree talk with the mango tree.

RESPONSE TO TREE TALK:

What actions will you take as a result of this tree talk? Or what decisions will you make?

TALK 3
THE MANGO TREE:
VALUE, VISION AND TRANSFORMATION

A clear vision, backed by definite plans, gives you a tremendous feeling of confidence and personal power.
—Brian Tracy

THE KING OF FRUITS

What is your favourite mango? This popular, delightful fruit comes in many sizes, shapes and brands. Mango is known as the "King of fruits and the fruit of passion, the love fruit. Mangoes are related to cashew and pistachios. Mangoes are nutritionally rich and provide 100% of your vitamin C and 12% of your daily fibre. I love mangoes and I have two Julie mango trees in my backyard that bear at least twice per year. This time of the year (summer) is especially fun for me because now I am in mango heaven in my backyard, and lately I have been seeing mangoes in a whole different light. They too have even been talking to me. No, I am not going bananas. The mangoes have been talking to me and teaching me powerful lessons on value, vision and transformation. I'll now share three of these powerful lessons with you.

Lesson 7: You are More Valuable than You Think; It's Based on What You See

When you look at a mango, what do you see? Many of us merely see a delightful, juicy and succulent fruit. However, some folks see a mango and see millions of dollars. How you may ask? Well while many persons eat the fruit and throw away the seeds, some will plant it and will have a tree that will produce more fruits. Mangoes can be used in salads, drinks and a host of other products. When some look at the mango, they see a juice company. They see bottles of drink and various outlets and franchises around the world. This is just one example but I am sure you get the point. How valuable are you? What abilities do you possess that you are not using or seeing? I pray you get a vision of your true value today!

Lesson 8: Transformation is a Process; Be Patient with Yourself

As I considered the Julie mango and really looked at it and the process of it becoming a tree and producing more fruits, I realized that transformation is a process. Even with the picture of the end in mind, a vision of what the mango can become, I realized it took time. The mango seed planted does not become a tree overnight nor does it take a few days or months. So it is with your vision of transformation. You have to see it and exercise patience and believe that though the vision may be delayed, it will come to pass.

LESSON 9: DON'T GIVE UP ON YOUR DREAM, EVEN WHEN IT SEEMS AS THOUGH NOTHING IS HAPPENING

Your vision is always for an appointed time or season in the future. My Julie mango tree does not bear all year round. When the seed was planted, it took a while before it emerged from the soil. It took a while as the tree grew and then later gained blossoms and started bearing fruit. While it was in the ground, although I could not see it, it had to be watered and I had to believe that it was developing. Something was happening. And so it is with your dream. The lesson therefore is: keep developing yourself. Don't give up. One day your dream will bear fruit. One day you will have your millions or whatever it is you are dreaming of or envisioning.

WHAT IS THE MANGO TREE SAYING TO YOU?

*Am I the only one to whom mangoes are talking? What are they saying to you? A major key to transformation is **YOU**. For things to change, you have to change. Transformation occurs when you change your thinking pattern and get a vision of your true worth. Be patient and persevere.*

Where there is a will, you'll definitely find a way. Stay tuned for tomorrow's tree talk with the mustard tree.

RESPONSE TO TREE TALK

What actions will you take as a result of this tree talk? Or what decisions will you make?

TALK 4
THE MUSTARD TREE:
GREAT ACHIEVEMENTS, SMALL BEGINNINGS

Success is the sum of small efforts—
repeated day in and day out
—Robert Collier

LOSING THE MUSTARD SEED

Many trees begin as seeds and over time they become towering figures, providing shade, fruit, food, shelter and a whole host of other uses and benefits essential to our survival on earth. It is simply just amazing when we realize what big things can emerge from small things. The parable of the mustard seed told by Jesus in Luke 13 has always been one of my favourites for encouragement along the Christian path.

"What is the Kingdom of God like? To what shall I compare it? It is like a grain of mustard seed, which a man took, and put in his own garden. It grew, and became a large tree, and the birds of the sky lodged in its branches." (Luke 13:18-19) I remember the day my first mentor, Bishop Neville Owens, showed me a mustard seed. I took it into my hand, shocked by its minuteness and before I could examine it well enough, it was nowhere to be found. This incident is forever etched in my mind. The mustard seed continues to shock me. How could such a tiny seed become a great useful tree? With this imagery and parable in mind, let's look at the lessons the mustard tree has on the path to transformation, personal development and success.

LESSON 10: DESPISE NOT SMALL BEGINNINGS ON THE JOURNEY TO SUCCESS

These proverbs all illustrate the first lesson. *"The journey to a thousand miles begins with the first step. By the yard it's hard but inch by inch it's a cinch."* How do you eat an elephant? The answer is: One bite at a time. When we look at our dreams, be it writing a book, owning a home, getting that degree, financial independence, expanding the business, etc, it can sometimes be overwhelming especially when all you have is an idea or limited resources. But the mustard seed reminds us that it is possible. If we start small and continue working, eventually we will realize the goal. Small steps eventually become big steps. There is a Jamaican proverb that points to this truth: "Every mickel, makes a muckle." If you save $1000 per week, by the end of the year that will be $52000. Imagine the returns in 10 or 15 years? If you write one page per day, by the end of the year, that's 365 pages and a big book. Will you take small steps on the journey towards your goal today? Let the mustard seed cheer you on your success journey today.

LESSON 11: SOW THE SEEDS TODAY FOR YOUR FUTURE SUCCESS

Seeds must be sown before they can become trees. As seeds are to trees so are ideas and thoughts to transformation and success. Stephen Covey in *The 7 Habits of Highly Effective People* aptly illustrates this second lesson: "sow a thought, reap an action; sow an action, reap a habit; sow a habit, reap a character; sow a character, reap a destiny." *Unless* you take action, nothing will happen. Your thoughts run your life. What thoughts and ideas are you sowing today? It's time to use your imagination and turn those ideas into action. Will you act on your ideas today and sow seeds for your future success?

LESSON 12: MY BEGINNING OR CURRENT STATE DOES NOT DICTATE OR DETERMINE MY END

The mustard seed was destined to become a great tree. Your current state is not a true reflection of your potential. Your true potential is what you were designed to do and become by the Great Intelligent Designer of the universe. What did the Creator and Divine Designer design for you to become when he created you? It's time to discover that design and bring it to life. Will you bring that design to life? Or will you stay stuck in your current condition? The mustard seed despite its size was destined for greatness and so are you despite your colour, class, race or current financial status. May the Creator give you insight into that design today, so that you will not remain a mustard seed but become a great tree with great benefits to those around you!

WHAT IS THE MUSTARD TREE SAYING TO YOU TODAY?

Are you small in your eyes? Do others see you as small? What is your true size? Great achievements can come from small beginnings. Despise not small beginnings. As seeds become great trees may you too become a great success.

Where there is a will, you'll definitely find a way. Stay tuned for tomorrow's tree talk with the pear tree.

RESPONSE TO TREE TALK

What actions will you take as a result of this tree talk? Or what decisions will you make?

TALK 5
THE PEAR TREE:
ACHIEVING GOALS

*Setting goals is the first step in turning
the invisible into the visible.*
—Anthony Robbins

MY WELCOME GIFT

In Jamaica we refer to the avocado tree as the pear tree. I love pears especially the dry ones. When I was living with my grandmother as a child, she had several pear trees on her property and where I currently reside we have a pear tree as do my neighbours. I still remember that day, in my first year in my current neighbourhood, when this nice, handsome, young man called from over the fence and offered me some wonderful pears. I was taken aback by his unexpected act of kindness which I suppose was his act of welcoming me to the neighbourhood. Back then the pear tree in my backyard was struggling to bear fruit and the tree itself was struggling for survival due to damage from storms and hurricanes. There was even a time when my landlady had to get a stick to support the tree but those struggling years now seem behind us and the tree has gotten stronger and is holding its own. Now as I write, my pear tree is bearing fruit and I have noticed some fascinating things which are now teaching me lessons on achieving goals and the pursuit of success.

LESSON 13: CONCEIVE AS MANY GOALS AS POSSIBLE; SOME MAY NOT MATERIALIZE BUT SOME WILL

The avocado tree typically can produce up to about one million flowers but will only typically set about 100 to 200 fruits per tree... or in other words, one (1) fruit in 10,000 will come to maturity. Sometimes they will set fruit but then drop them when they are pea sized... again this is typical. The habit of the pear tree to drop many of its young fruit caught my attention as I swept. I had also noticed that a similar thing had happened with the Julie mango tree. It was then that the pear tree spoke. "Not every goal you conceive will be accomplished. Not every book idea will become a book but some will."

Some people tend not to want to dream because sometimes their dreams do not materialize. I do not believe this is sufficient reason not to dream or set goals. Should the pear tree no longer produce flowers and fruits because of the high numbers of pears which will not reach maturity? If it had that attitude then I could not enjoy its fruit. This also should be our attitude; press towards our goals no matter what. Do you have a list of 50 goals, that is, things you would like to be, do, have or see; places you would like to go and the contribution you would like to make before you die? I do. If you aim at nothing, you will miss one hundred percent of the time but if you aim at something chances are at some point in time you will hit the target and who knows what may happen when you do!

LESSON 14: DON'T STRESS YOURSELF TOO MUCH WHEN A GOAL DOES NOT MATERIALIZE; SET NEW ONES

The question has been asked: "What can be done to minimize fruit drop of good "fertilized" pear fruit? The answer I found was quite interesting. "Avoid stressing the tree, that is, don't under or overwater the tree." Imagine that! What if we all could take that attitude to life? I remember my two broken engagements, when twice my hopes for marriage were dashed, they were devastating experiences! Hope deferred makes the heart sick and indeed I even got physically sick but I was determined not to crumble and give up. I still have hopes of getting married. I learnt during that time that it was not the experience so much that made me sick, it was not the stressor but my response to the stress. Many studies have proven this fact.

In fact, sometimes it is stressing that often causes our goals to be cut short. We may self sabotage due to past experiences. Attitude determines altitude and with respect to achieving our goals, a good attitude of perseverance goes a long way. It took Thomas Edison 10,000 attempts before he created the incandescent light bulb. Sir Richard Charles Nicholas Branson is an English businessman and investor. He is best known as the founder of Virgin Group, which comprises more than 400 companies but along the way he had a myriad of business failures. He notes: "For every success story there's 100s of near-misses. Every entrepreneur fails before succeeding."[1]

JK Rowling, mega successful author of the Harry Potter series was turned down by more than 10 publishers before securing a book deal, only then to be told to get a part time job as there is no money in children's books. Jack Canfield originator of Chicken Soup for the Soul series was rejected by more than 130 publishers but he persevered until a small, self-help publisher in Florida called HCI2 published the work. Chicken Soup for the Soul eventually became a major best seller with a book series of over 250 titles has sold more than 110 million copies in the U.S. and Canada. Chicken Soup for the Soul books have been translated into 43 languages, have been published in over 100 countries, and have sold more than 500 million copies worldwide.[3] Jack Canfield holds the *Guinness Book World Record* for having seven books simultaneously on the *New York Times Bestseller List*. He also holds the *Guinness Book World Record* for the largest book-signing ever for *Chicken Soup for the Kid's Soul.*

LESSON 15: BUILD A NETWORK OF SUPPORTERS TO HELP YOU TO ACHIEVE YOUR GOALS

There has been research in Israel which suggests that fruit retention is also facilitated when there are other avocado varieties present to provide cross-pollination and that these crossed fruit have a higher tendency to stay on the tree.[4] The lesson here is that no one succeeds alone and for us to have lasting results, we need to be part of a network. One of my favourite African proverbs solidifies this point. "If you want to go fast, go alone. If you want to go far, go together." Team work makes the dream work. "If two lie down together, they will be warm, but a person alone will not be warm. An enemy might defeat one person, but two people together can defend themselves; a rope that is woven of three strings is hard to break." (Ecclesiastes 4:11-12). Encouragement sweetens labour. Even the Lord Jesus did not try to go it alone. He chose twelve apostles at the start of his ministry and sent them and other disciples on various missions in teams, two by two in several instances. Napoleon Hill who studied the success of hundreds of men over 25 years, calls this key to success, a mastermind alliance. If we have support when the times get rough we can stay the course and achieve the goal. Whom do you have as support? Where is your team? If you don't have one, it's time to take initiative and build one so you can increase the chances of achieving your goals.

WHAT IS THE PEAR TREE SAYING TO YOU?

What is the pear tree saying to you about your goals? Will you conceive many goals? Will you continue to aim for your goals in the face of repeated failures? Will you build a team to increase your chances of success?

Where there is a will, you'll definitely find a way. Stay tuned for tomorrow's tree talk with the lime tree.

RESPONSE TO TREE TALK

What actions will you take as a result of this tree talk? Or what decisions will you make?

TALK 6
THE LIME TREE:
TRANSITION, NEW
BEGINNINGS AND
EXPANSION

*There are far better things ahead
than any we leave behind.*
—C.S. Lewis

THE GLORY DAYS

Every so often I have the privilege of sharing with others some of the limes from the lime tree in my backyard. This lime tree is special because it produces large limes. My landlady has often told me stories of the days when the yields were tremendous. She would see people buying these tiny limes and then give them some of her limes. Nevertheless, in recent years, the yield has not been as great and the tree is not producing limes the size of its glorious past.

However, every so often I get a glimpse of what it used to be like when I find some unusually large limes on the tree. Despite these glimpses my landlady does not believe it will return to its glory days and as such she has planted a new lime tree in the backyard. That tree has not produced any yield yet and while we wait, we continue to enjoy what's left of this old tree which is at least 10 years old. The fact that she did not cut it down continues to fascinate me and as I observed the trees that morning while raking the yard, the lime tree spoke to me, giving vital lessons on transitions, expansions and new beginnings.

LESSON 16: DO NOT WAIT UNTIL A TREE DIES BEFORE PLANTING A NEW ONE

This lesson can be applied easily to making transitions in a number of areas but more so with our career pursuits. I remember Jim Rohn speaking on the value of working part-time on your dream while working full-time on your job. He worked part-time on his fortune until his part-time investments started paying more than his full-time job and then he made the part-time full-time. The days of the gold watch are over, where you stay on one job until retirement and get a gold watch. Job security is not guaranteed in today's climate especially if you work with technology which keeps changing. Our society now demands lifelong learning and people change careers more often.

We, however, must be careful how we make the transitions. We must be clear on our next steps before we decide to move on. The proverb of not throwing away the baby with the bath water accurately reflects this lesson. We should always be on the lookout for new opportunities for greater yields and invest in personal development. Rohn emphasises: "Work harder on yourself than you do on your job." You may lose your job but your value and skills will remain and you can always apply elsewhere for another job. Do not wait until you are fired before you start thinking about the future. Invest in more than one skill set so if one fails you have something to fall back on.

LESSON 17: WHILE NEW BEGINNINGS MAY BE NECESSARY, THEY MUST BE PURSUED WISELY

People start over for many reasons. Perhaps like my lime tree the yields are no longer satisfactory. Sometimes a market dries up, a product is no longer needed, a business closes down, you get fired or injured etc. Sometimes a particular career is no longer as satisfactory or fulfilling as we had expected and sometimes we find that perhaps we were labouring in the wrong place. Have you ever seen persons trained in a particular field who are not working in that field? This has happened to me three times. I believe each career path served its purpose for a season. Like the decision taken by my landlady, it was time to plant a new lime tree in a different location to eventually produce greater yields.

However I did not cut down the old tree immediately. At times I did both things until it was clear that I had to make a choice and work in one field. For example, I taught part-time while I served as a missionary until it was felt that my missionary yields were not sufficient because it demanded a full-time focus. The new path was challenging. I knew that it would be costly and required faith for daily survival but in the end I learnt so much and found the experience very valuable. It also expanded my horizon, resulting in a web of influence in more than 30 countries around the world. Imagine if I had merely been teaching in the classroom, I could not have had that global impact in such a short time. The lesson I learnt in all of this was that we must consider the cost before starting over. The new beginning whether forced or intentional must be undertaken properly and wisely.

Lesson 18: Do not be Afraid to Expand Your Horizons to Increase Your Yields

In our backyard we now have two lime trees in two different locations. Perhaps my landlady will cut down the old one or perhaps she will let it remain. But what she has done speaks profoundly to me and recently we also gave away some seedlings to a friend of mine who lives in another parish. Both acts speak volumes to me. We must seek new opportunities to expand and increase our yields. This applies to many fields even in Christendom. Jesus told his followers to make disciples of all nations, to go into all the world to spread his teachings.

Unfortunately, many of us are not prepared to do the work it takes for expansion. When books are translated into many languages it is putting this lesson into action. It is one way of increasing the yield. The same can be applied to music and many other fields. In the field of athletics, I notice in addition to local track meets there are the World Championships, the Olympics, the CARIFTA games, the Penn Relays and the Diamond League events. These events give athletes opportunities to expand their horizons and also result in more income for them. Will you make a decision to increase your yields today? How will you expand to increase your yields? Do not just sell your product in Jamaica or your home country. Do not just have one tree in one location! Don't settle for the expected. Be strategic.

Explore new options. Expand and increase your yields!

WHAT IS THE LIME TREE SAYING TO YOU?

Is it time to plant a new tree? Is it time to invest in a new skill, to invest in your personal development? Is it time to expand your horizon or to start over? Whatever you choose to do, do it wisely and count the cost.

Where there is a will, you will definitely find a way. Stay tuned for tomorrow's tree talk with the moringa tree.

RESPONSE TO TREE TALK

What actions will you take as a result of this tree talk? Or what decisions will you make?

TALK 7
THE MORINGA TREE:
CLUELESS TO THE SEEDS
OF SUCCESS

*Your diamonds are not in far
distant mountains or in yonder
seas; they are in your own
backyard, if you but dig for them.*
—Russell H. Conwell
Acres of Diamonds

A DANCE OR A SEED?

"MERENGUE, MERENGUE," shouted the Rasta man in Half Way Tree, Kingston, Jamaica. Being a teacher of Latin American culture, those words reminded me of a Latino dance and thus I looked around expectantly to see a dance but did not see anyone dancing. What I did see were some funny looking seeds in his hand and then figured out that he was not talking about the rhythmic, sexy, Latino dance from the Dominican Republic. He was in fact selling seeds from the **moringa** tree. It was a classic case of another Jamaican habit of mispronouncing the names of things or a foreign language interference problem.

Notwithstanding, I had no clue what moringa was or its importance until I landed in Zambia, Africa. It was while I was there in 2013, that I was introduced first hand to the moringa tree and the wonderful benefits of this so called **miracle** tree. It was there my interest peaked and only to discover ironically that for three years the same kind of tree was in my backyard and I was clueless about it and had never used it. Now that is incredible! It got me thinking what else do you or I have in our backyards which is of great benefit, -that we are clueless about? Are we sitting on millions or something that could make a huge difference to our lives and the lives of others and are clueless about it? This revelation was proven when I was introduced to the Jamaican Green Smoothie movement founded by my friend Didan Ashanta.

Jamaican Green Smoothies

In 2013, Didan blogged about Green Smoothies and the need to find ingredients that the average Jamaican could easily find and use especially those we often grow in our backyards. She wanted to show that the green smoothie habit could be an affordable, easy and delicious way to consume those healthy leafy greens that we don't like to eat. For those who are not aware, a green smoothie is not the same as a green juice. It is beverage that is made from a blend of leafy greens (like Lettuce or Callaloo), fruits (like Banana or Mango) and liquids (like Water or Coconut Milk).

Didan started the Jamaican Green Smoothie movement because many of the ingredients pre-scribed in regular smoothies are often foreign to us Jamaicans. To facilitate the habit, she began a 30 day Jamaican Green Smoothie challenge. It was then that my backyard became more meaningful. With great excitement, I researched the uses of moringa and found out some amazing things about this miracle tree. The uses are tantalizing. Every part of the tree can be used in medicine. I was fascinated! Moringa oleifera has an impressive range of medicinal uses with high nutritional value and medicinal benefits. Different parts of moringa contain a profile of important minerals and are a good source of protein, vitamins, beta-carotene, amino acids and various phenolics. Moringa can act as cardiac and circulatory stimulants, possess antitumor, antipyretic, antiepileptic, anti-inflammatory, antiulcer, antispasmodic, diuretic, antihypertensive, cholesterol lowering, antioxidant, antidiabetic, hepatoprotective, antibacterial and antifungal activities, and are being employed for the treatment of different ailments in the indigenous system of medicine. Traditional cultures in various parts of the world have long used moringa in their herbal medicine repertoire for ailments ranging from gout to various inflammations and fevers.[5]

MORINGA EXPERIMENTS

One day my landlady mentioned cutting down the moringa tree in our backyard. I told her absolutely no! This tree has too many benefits and besides it was benefitting me greatly. As my discoveries continued, I started moringa experiments and the moringa leaves became the main leafy green in my smoothies over the 30 day challenge. My first experiment with moringa was the making of my first green smoothie: a combination of fresh green moringa leaves, ripe banana and water and it was oh so delicious! This led to further cooking experiments such as moringa rice (similar to callaloo rice); moringa stew, moringa chop suey with chicken breasts. Then I began ingesting the seeds for weight loss and a boost in my energy levels. I also began recommending moringa to my friends and giving them gifts of moringa leaves and seeds.

My experience with the moringa tree has taught me valuable lessons and poses a challenge to us all. How many of us have some awesome gifts and other things in our backyard but do not know it? Sometimes we may even be getting rid of something that is extremely valuable because we do not know the value. Are you clueless to the seeds of success within you? If you are, please take these three lessons below to heart.

LESSON 19: BECOME MORE AWARE OF WHAT YOU HAVE WITHIN; SEARCH YOUR OWN 'BACKYARD' FOR GIFTS AND TALENTS

The moringa tree was there all along but I did not recognize it or know its worth, its value and its uses. Within many of us are ideas that could be life transforming, ideas that could change the world, ideas that could make us millionaires but when you don't know who you are, and you don't take the time to search within, you could, in fact, miss the ideas for success or even get rid of that which will be valuable to your success. The seeds of success are already planted within you by the Creator and Divine Designer of the universe. If we are going to be successful we must look within and see what has been deposited. We must explore our own backyards and become more aware of what is in it if we want to achieve success.

LESSON 20: EVERY BUSINESS OR INVENTION IS A SOLUTION TO A PROBLEM TO BENEFIT OTHERS

It was only after I studied the moringa tree and realized its benefits that I started experimenting with it and sharing the benefits with others. I could not make full use of the tree or help anyone if I remained ignorant about its uses and had been unwilling to experiment. Zig Ziglar often said, if you help enough people to achieve their goals you will eventually get yours. In order to help others, you must have something to offer. In order to have something to offer, you should study your gifts, become more self aware and begin to think of the ways you can use that which you possess to benefit and help others. These are key elements of success.

LESSON 21: BE WILLING TO EXPERIMENT; YOU NEVER KNOW WHAT YOU MAY INVENT OR DISCOVER

I was amazed at the dishes I could create with moringa. Who knows if my moringa chop suey or moringa rice might become a hit? The moringa tree has sure saved me money and helped me to consume more healthy drinks and meals. Had I not experimented I would have missed out. It's not enough to be aware of what's in your backyard. It's not enough to have an idea. You need to act on it and experiment. Experimentation leads to inventions and inventions marketed and used well can lead to huge financial success or extraordinary breakthroughs that may transform lives globally.

WHAT IS THE MORINGA TREE SAYING TO YOU?

Do you know what's in your backyard? Are you aware of the talents hidden within you? Are you studying the backyard of your mind and heart? Are you experimenting with ideas?

Where there is a will, you will definitely find a way. Stay tuned for tomorrow's tree talk with the palm tree.

RESPONSE TO TREE TALK

What actions will you take as a result of this tree talk? Or what decisions will you make?

TALK 8
THE PALM TREE:
BEATING THE ODDS

Adversity is the mother of progress.
—Mahatma Gandhi

MY AFRO-EUROPEAN
EXPERIENCE

I live on the beautiful paradise isle of Jamaica. My island is known as the land of wood and water. Trees are therefore in abundance and they are mostly green all year round. So imagine my shock when I went to Germany in the dead of winter and saw trees without leaves. It was the strangest thing ever! On the converse side, imagine my shock when I went to Namibia, Africa, in what is often considered the summer months (July - August) in the Western Hemisphere and almost everything was brown!

Green was a scarcity in Namibia, a desert land, but the acacia trees and some other evergreens managed to reflect some green hope. Rainfall was a rarity making the land arid and parched. The few trees with green leaves brought me to a state of feeling homesick. In fact the impact was far more profound than I had realized and what happened on returning to Jamaica showcased that impact. I certainly was not prepared emotionally for what happened on returning to Jamaica after 10 weeks on African soil.

Shortly before the plane landed at the Norman Manley airport in Kingston, the sight of the greenery on my paradise isle brought tears to my eyes. Yes, I was moved to tears by the greenery and a most breath taking green view of my island! Perhaps it was at that point that my love for trees was rekindled. Perhaps it was at that moment the trees took a liking to me and decided to start having conversations with me. From then on evergreen trees have become a fascination and it gives me great joy to have an evergreen in my backyard: the magnificent palm. I'm really excited to share three lessons from the evergreen palm tree especially since the land of wood and water is currently experiencing drought and the magnificent palm seems unaffected.

LESSON 22: STAY GREEN; THIS IS A SYMBOL OF STABILITY, GROWTH AND ENDURANCE

Green is said to symbolize life, renewal, nature, energy, growth, harmony, freshness, safety, fertility, and the environment. This color is also traditionally associated with money, finances, healing, rest and relaxation. Green can help enhance vision, stability and endurance. The color green affects us physically and mentally in several different ways. Green is soothing, relaxing, and youthful. Green is a color that helps alleviate anxiety, depression, and nervousness. Green also brings with it a sense of hope, health, adventure, and renewal, as well as self-control, compassion and harmony.[6]

Evergreens stay green all year because they have tough, tightly wrapped, leather-like leaves or needles that are not prone to drying out like the leaves of other trees. Since evergreens have small, wrapped leaves, it leads to less moisture loss. Evergreen tree leaves have a wax like coating that absorb moisture. This storage of moisture means they can survive with no sunlight because when the temperature gets colder or drier, plants are unable to draw liquid water from the soil. An equally important factor is that evergreens produce chlorophyll all year long. Chlorophyll is the pigment that makes leaves green and that which helps plants to produce food.

In order for us to stay green, we need to feed or nourish ourselves well. We need to establish protective structures or enclaves to guard against "drying it." This means we need nourishment physically, mentally and spiritually. Jesus once said that man cannot live by bread alone but by words. Nourishment of the mind is important for success. We should nourish it with a healthy dose of positive things on a daily basis. I practice listening to motivational messages daily and also read my bible and other positive reading materials to nourish my mind.

As for the food, we all know the benefits of eating the right foods for good health. If we are to stay green like the palm tree we need to ensure that we are fed well spiritually, physically and mentally. This further means monitoring the influences around us and reducing or eliminating things that are toxic to our growth. Sometimes this means limiting time with certain friends and family members, reducing the flow of their negative energy so we can maintain our moisture of positivity in order to stay green.

LESSON 23: DO NOT ALLOW THE EXTERNAL SITUATIONS OR CONDITIONS TO ROB YOU OF ACHIEVING YOUR GOAL

In the book of Jeremiah, God compares the one who trusts in him to an evergreen tree. Such trees are not affected by drought or the heat of summer (Jeremiah 17:7-8). The palm tree does not allow the external situations to affect its internal programming, to inhibit its goal of blooming and staying green. It stays green regardless of the weather conditions. That's a huge lesson in itself on personal development and the journey to success.

I believe too often we allow the external circumstances to affect us internally, to mess up our minds so that we cannot function and cannot produce or develop as we should. The palm tree is an exceptional example of learning to bloom where you are planted. I implore you, do not permit the negative external elements or lack of supply to inhibit your growth and development. Do not allow the negative externals to rob you of opportunities to achieve your goals and your mission in life. Focus like the palm tree on blooming and remaining green. Learn ways to adapt. Be flexible. If one thing does not work, try another. Do not let external situations affect your output to the point where they destroy your goals and ruin your plans for success.

LESSON 24: KEEP VICTORY IN YOUR MIND'S EYE; ACT AS IF YOU CANNOT FAIL

In Christian iconography as well as in ancient times, palm trees symbolized victory, triumph and goodness. What would you dare to do if you knew you could not fail? What if you acted as if you could never fail, as if failure were not an option? Every athlete trains with victory in mind. Every athlete aims to finish well and to finish first. Athletes keep their eyes on the prize and pay the price of gruelling training to meet that goal. That's the attitude we should have on the journey to success.

Our first Jamaican, national hero, Marcus Mosiah Garvey puts it well: "If you have no confidence in self, you are twice defeated in the race of life." This is the winning attitude. Thomas Edison had it and that's why he created the light bulb on the 10,000th attempt. Grandma Cha Sa-soon had it and that is why she passed her driver's license test on the 950th attempt. In the Christian faith, Christians are reminded that they are more than conquerors through Jesus their Lord. Be like the palm in the drought! Don't let the drought or the cold defeat you! Determine to triumph in your situation. It's not over until you win!

WHAT IS THE MAGNIFICENT PALM TREE SAYING TO YOU?

Are you determined to stay green like the palm tree? Are you determined to beat the odds and flourish despite the drought or cold? What will you do to nourish and protect yourself so that your goals will materialize? What would you dare to do if you knew you could not fail? Will you operate with a victorious mindset and be determined to win?

Where there is a will, you will definitely find a way. Stay tuned for tomorrow's tree talk with the banana tree.

RESPONSE TO TREE TALK

What actions will you take as a result of this tree talk? Or what decisions will you make?

TALK 9
THE BANANA TREE:
SUPPORT AND SUCCESSION PLANNING

*Great things in business are never
done by one person. They're done
by a team of people.
—Steve Jobs*

GOING BANANAS

I'm finally going bananas! Yes I am! This should really not surprise you because I did mention before that I am from the banana parish of St Mary, Jamaica. I have lived with banana trees for most of my life since childhood so no wonder I am finally going bananas! I love bananas and in particular, ripe bananas. Ripe bananas have many health benefits and some even say a banana a day is more powerful than an apple a day.

The parish of my birth is known for St. Mary's banana chips but I also remember those *dukoonoos* or *"blue draws"* my grandmother used to make using banana leaves. This is dough made of cornmeal well seasoned and cooked in banana leaves. I loved it! I also remember making a head rest (khata) from dried banana leaves; this is used to rest the pot or pans on the head as we travelled from one point to another with such loads. Younger Jamaicans or those from the city would not know about these things. Khatas helped us to carry loads on our heads.

My mom even remembers banana trash being used as stuffing for her bed. I bet you never knew the banana tree had such fascinating uses! Studying bananas is no monkey business! Banana leaves can be fed to horses, cows and other grazers. The dried remains of the trunks can be used for weaving baskets and mats. Besides these uses, the banana trees in my backyard have been talking to me about relationships, support systems and succession planning. So let's dive into these three lessons as we learn more about the fascinating banana tree.

Lesson 25: Establish Your Support System; You Cannot Successfully Bear Fruit or the Loads of Life Alone

Two banana trees in my backyard have fallen. Another two are bent and my landlady has had to get sticks to hold them up to keep them from toppling over. One of those bent banana trees is bearing fruit. Banana trees need support to successfully bear fruit. It cannot bear the load of its fruit alone. Bananas start life very, very straight but as the bunch emerges from the top of the plant and the bracts roll back (bracts are the leathery purple things that separate the hands of bananas) and fall off, the bananas begin to spread out and turn upward. They do this because bananas are negatively geo-tropic. This means that they grow away from the pull of gravity, as opposed to turning upward toward the sun.[7]

We, like the banana tree, need a support system and the stronger the better. Every corporation needs a strong support system via its network of employees and leadership. Every successful business has strong support systems. Every successful leader has strong support systems. The question is: do you have the support you need? How is your support system? Some of us have retreated into ourselves because of hurt and have cut ourselves off from the support systems of friends and family relationships.

Through my trials and heartaches I learnt the value of having a strong support system or the need for social support. Had it not been for family and friends, I would not have survived two broken engagements and two health crises where my lung collapsed. Had it not been for my support systems, I would have not travelled to several different countries and sent many Jamaicans across the world to make a difference among the poor and marginalized. Also I would not have written and published my first book and other accomplishments. We are not meant to carry our loads alone. We are not meant to succeed alone. We all need support.

LESSON 26: GIVE YOURSELF ROOM TO GROW IN THE RIGHT ENVIRONMENT OR SOIL

Banana plants like rich, dark, fertile soil; lots of mulch and organic matter; lots of nitrogen and potassium (chicken manure); steady warmth, not too hot and not too cold. The temperature needs to be just right. They need steady moisture, in the ground and in the air. They also need good shelter if they are to thrive and successfully bear fruit. Banana plants dislike strong winds, extreme heat or cold; being hungry or thirsty; being alone and exposed. If you intend to grow bananas, you need to know these things.

The question is: do you know what you need to grow and develop, to release the treasure that is within you and to live the life you were designed to live? What is the best environment for your growth? Is your current environment causing you to grow or is it toxic? Do you know your likes and dislikes? If not, it's time to do some serious evaluation and introspection or seek help. You may need to change friends, change address, change careers, change jobs, change countries. Perhaps it's time to seek a coach or mentor or to enrol in a personal development program. Whatever the case, like the banana tree, you need the right environment to bear fruit or you will fall and die prematurely before you have borne fruit.

LESSON 27: LEAVE A SUCCESSOR; WHEN THE BANANA TREE IS READY TO DIE, IT SHOOTS

The mark of true leadership is having successors. You have not done a good job if no one is able to carry on after you are gone. The mission must continue. The intention should always be to bear fruit that remains, that is lasting fruit. That's why trees reproduce. Jesus, the master teacher of success, did this at the start of his ministry. He selected leaders and spent time training and developing them to take over.

Today we see the results of that initiative because Christianity has become a global religion. We see the examples and need for succession planning in many key areas of life. This is the reason we have children for the posterity of the human race. This is the reason we leave an inheritance. The wise person leaves an inheritance for his children's children.

Is succession planning foremost in your mind? Perhaps unlike Jesus, you did not begin your ministry, business or organization with this in mind, but it's never too late to start. Who will you train to take over? What values do you want to pass on to the next generation? What ideas will outlive you? What materials will you create to pass on value to the next generation?

WHAT IS THE BANANA TREE SAYING TO YOU?

Do you have a support system? How strong is it? Who is helping you to bear the loads of life? Are you trying to succeed alone? Do you have a plan for succession? Do you have room to grow in your current environment?

Where there is a will, you will definitely find a way. Stay tuned for tomorrow's tree talk with the starfruit tree.

RESPONSE TO TREE TALK

What actions will you take as a result of this tree talk? Or what decisions will you make?

TALK 10
THE STARFRUIT TREE:
RELEASING THE STAR IN YOU

*Productivity is never an accident. It
is always the result of commitment
to excellence, intelligent planning
and focussed effort.*
—*Paul J. Myer*

MY NEIGHBOUR'S STARFRUIT

I've always been fascinated by the Carambola also
known as Starfruit or Chinese Gimbelin. My neighbour has a tree and every time I see it I am
challenged. The tree is fruitful all year round. This
has been my observation for the past five years.
Now it makes me ask myself: what can I produce or
do that will generate cash flow or income like my
neighbour's starfruit? It seems our Creator has giv-
en the starfruit tree a secret for ongoing productivity
that we need to learn if we are going to release our
inner star. Whatever the case, the tree is a visible
reminder of what our Divine Designer intended for
us when he blessed the first humans and said: "Be
fruitful." There are also three life lessons that the
tree can teach us to fuel our success and release
our inner star.

LESSON 28: BE UNSTOPPABLE

A star may be defined as someone who plays a leading role in a movie or someone who is highly celebrated in a particular field. In the movies, the star or protagonist usually wins no matter how bad it is or how bad it gets. S/he is unstoppable. Not only is the Carambola fruit shaped like a star when cut but this tree is also truly a star of fruit bearing. It is like an unstoppable movie star, producing fruit every day no matter what. No wonder it is called **Starfruit**.

In the same way, in order for us to be successful we have to become a star in our field. We have to become valuable and develop sufficient mastery that we attract attention and investors. Jim Rohn said it well, "Success is something you attract by what you become." Become a person who produces great results, who bears fruit continually in your endeavours like the starfruit. Let nothing hinder you. Don't be caught up with activities, it is the results that matter. Ongoing and unstoppable productivity is the aim of the game. There is a starfruit tree in you. Plant the seed and let it grow. There are starfruit like ideas in your mind and heart. Produce the ideas and let them multiply and give you ongoing fruit. You have a star product inside you. Mass produce it and reap success. There is a star in you. Give birth to your star and let it shine today!

LESSON 29: BE CONSISTENT IN YOUR ACTIONS

The starfruit tree is consistent in its output. Consistency is a key to success. If a company does not produce consistently, it cannot stay in business. It has to maintain the consistency of production in quality and quantity to meet the demands of the market. We too must be consistent in words and actions. Consistency leads to dependability and reliability. Consistency speaks of certainty and builds trust. Our values must be consistent and our performance ought to be consistent. Consistency is the key to building your brand or reputation. KFC tastes the same wherever I buy it. If your product is not consistent in its quality you will lose customers. It's the same with your life. Your consistent actions or habits shape your destiny. Are you being consistent with the right things or the wrong things? It's time to evaluate your habits. It's time to develop a measure of consistency and develop winning habits to foster ongoing productivity like the starfruit tree. Consistency is vital to releasing your inner star.

LESSON 30: BE FOCUSSED

This is the age of distraction. The primary sources are social media, emails, cell phones, games, youtube, parties and the list goes on and on. Irrespective of the external situations or weather conditions, the starfruit tree remains fixed on producing fruit. In the last five years, I have never seen a day that it had no fruit even when we experienced a drought. Focus is a major key to success. When we focus, our productivity increases. When we take time to focus and think, especially in solitude, incredible ideas and answers to questions emerge. I've proven this time and time again.

I heard Brian Tracy in two presentations, tell the story that when he asked the two richest men in the world, Bill Gates and Warren Buffet, for their number one key to success, that each of them replied almost simultaneously saying: "focus." We cannot be a jack of all trades and master of none. Every star and person of renown is famous or known primarily for one thing. Usain Bolt is known for running; Bob Marley is known for music; Bill Gates for Microsoft; Steve Jobs is known for Apple products; Mother Theresa is known for caring for the poor and Nelson Mandela for fighting against apartheid. The question is what are you known for? What's your starfruit? What do you want to be known for? Whatever you focus the most on, that is what you will manifest or produce.

WHAT IS THE STARFRUIT TREE SAYING TO YOU?

What will you create that will produce ongoing fruit or income? What is your starfruit? In order to release the star in you, it will require ongoing productivity which leads to success. You will need to be unstoppable in your pursuit, consistent in your actions and remain focused. It's time to release the star in you.

Where there is a will, you'll definitely find a way. Stay tuned for tomorrow's tree talk as we begin a series of life lessons on personal and financial growth.

RESPONSE TO TREE TALK

What actions will you take as a result of this tree talk? Or what decisions will you make?

PART II:
GROW LIKE TREES

*A people without the knowledge of
their past history, origin and
culture is like a tree without roots.
—Marcus Garvey*

Recording My Tree Talks

TALK 11
MOM'S STORY:
SUCCESS AFTER 38 YEARS

Hungry mek monkey blow fire.
(People are forced to become innovative
and resourceful under harsh conditions)
[Jamaican Proverb]

The pursuit of a dream is often like an odyssey with its many twists and turns. It is very much like the process of growing strong trees. Strong trees do not grow overnight. Strong trees have weathered many storms and today they stand tall having withstood the tests of life. They are a reminder that no matter how bad it is or how bad it gets we should rise above the adversities and stand tall. The series of talks in this section speak to growing like trees and what better way to motivate you than to share the story of my mother, whose success came after 38 years of chasing a childhood dream. She has grown much like a tree and today she stands tall like a strong cedar tree.

My mother is my role model and motivator when the road seems tough and my dreams seem elusive and that is why this book is dedicated to her. In my presentations to parents, I often speak to them about my mom's tremendous spirit of perseverance and tenacity and the ways in which she has weathered many storms like the palm tree and is now flourishing. Today, I will share my mom's story and highlight three attitudes that we must possess if we are to grow like strong trees and achieve success.

This is the story of a Jamaican woman who refused to give up on her childhood dream. How many of you remember as a child being asked the question: What do you want to be when you grow up? Well Marva, my mom, remembers that at the age of eight she wanted to become a **Registered Nurse** and graduate from the University of the West Indies but a major obstacle stood between her and her dream: poverty. Life was difficult as she was the 5th of 9 children being raised by a single mother in a poor rural agricultural district in St. Mary. In fact, her family was so poor that people in the district expected very little of them and some community members even remarked that she would never amount to anything good. Mom, however, took these words to heart and was determined to prove them wrong.

EDUCATIONAL CHALLENGES AND THE DREAM

Mom was very intelligent and paid careful attention in school. Despite not having lunch on many school days, she would not be deterred from attending school and she worked hard. My grandmother worked on a banana plantation but the money she earned was not enough to send all her children to school at once. Nevertheless, when most children opted to stay home from school on Fridays, which was the norm in mom's hometown, mom ensured she didn't because Friday was the day when the principal would ask current affairs questions during devotion. If you got them right, then you would win books, pencils and so on. That was one of the ways that my mother got things for school. These came in handy and mom worked hard. Her hard work was not in vain and she won a place at a new High School, Jose Marti Technical, but once again, poverty prevented her from seizing this opportunity. Disappointed but determined Mom remained in Mount Angus All Age School and eventually gained a place at another school: Guys Hill Secondary. Since my grandmother still could not afford it, Mom asked her neighbour to help to make her uniform (the neighbour's child was attending the institution). This time she was determined to seize the offer and it was here that her entrepreneurial skills began to surface as she would sell coconut oil and oranges and mom saved every penny she earned to send herself to school.

However, the distance to travel to school began to take its toll. Unlike Mount Angus, Guy's Hill was nine miles away and if she missed the bus or could not find the money to pay the fare, she would have to walk to school. When she was in grade eight, the principal allowed her to move in with her. It made life easier. However, this good fortune did not immediately propel mom any step closer to achieving her dream. Lady Misfortune presented herself through peer pressure and at the age of 17, mom found herself socially embarrassed, ashamed and dejected. She became pregnant with me, her first child. It was a devastating blow!

At first Mom was just in denial. She did not know what to do. She thought about abortion and wondered how my grandmother would react. When she finally told my grandmother, to say my grandmother was disappointed is an understatement -she was enraged. Mom recalled getting punished severely and grandma telling her that she had no intention of helping her to raise a child. After giving birth to me, mom did whatever she had to make ends meet. She went back to grating coconuts to make coconut oil, and also received some help from my paternal grandmother who encouraged her to efmigrate to the city so she could have a better life. Thus at the age of two, we were separated as mom left St Mary to better herself and left me in the care of my paternal family in another parish.

PREGNANCIES AND THE PURSUIT OF A BETTER LIFE

Despite the setback and the disruption of education, with this blessing, her hope of achieving her dream was renewed. Mom moved to the city of Kingston in search of a better life and this move landed her in the Inner City of Olympic Gardens. Life in Kingston was not easy because Mom was unskilled and securing a good and stable job was challenging. Mom, however, was very teachable and good mannered and these traits brought more blessings. She found a home with some kind strangers who encouraged her and helped her to get a fresh start. Nevertheless five years later, my sister was born and a year later my brother was born and this time around, there were no relatives to help but mom did her best to care for her three children.

Mom being very teachable and hardworking, was determined to overcome her circumstances, and over the next thirteen years held several jobs. She worked in the garment factories and quickly learnt the skill of a seamstress. She employed her entrepreneurial skills by selling goods and produce at

Coronation market; she sold juices at the gate of primary schools and did the same at home. Eventually she got married and became a **practical nurse** and for a while all her effort and investment were focused on caring for and educating her three children. By this time all three children were living with her in Olympic Gardens and in due course she gained steady employment at the Kingston Public Hospital (KPH) as a Ward Assistant.

THE TURNING POINT

One fateful afternoon, at a parent teachers' meeting at my High school, Meadowbrook High, a presenter challenged the parents to not only invest in their children but to also invest in themselves and not to give up on their dreams. The speaker said that they should never use their children as an excuse to not further themselves. They must never blame their children for not being able to achieve their personal dreams but should work simultaneously with them to improve themselves. Mom took what the presenter said to heart and at the age of 37 decided to once again pursue her childhood dream of becoming a **Registered Nurse**.

This was no easy feat because Mom had no CXC subjects and the requirement was 5 CXC subjects including Mathematics and English but Mom was determined to succeed this time. Thus Mom worked and attended evening classes for three of the subjects and taught herself two of the subjects. Math and English were very challenging. After four attempts she passed Math and after at least 7 attempts she passed English. Her hard work and determination had paid off and finally she was able to enrol in Brown's Town Community College to pursue a Bachelor of Science in Nursing at the age of 43.

SUCCESS AT LAST

Fortunately for Mom, the community college had a partnership with the University of the West Indies and this was the second batch pursuing this degree. Previously, nurses after three years would graduate with a diploma but Mr. Blessing had yet again smiled upon her. Although life as a student was challenging those three years, with faith in God, a good attitude and hard work, Mom graduated with second class honours as a **Registered Nurse** with a Bachelor of Science in Nursing. You should have seen how mom and my grandmother proudly walked the campus of the University of the West Indies to celebrate! **Finally after 38 years, at the age of 46, Mom's childhood dream had become a reality!** Mom created history at Kingston Public Hospital as the first Ward Assistant to move from that position to become a registered nurse with a degree. She had after 38 years defied the odds and silenced the naysayers but the story did not end there.

Within three years Mom improved on her qualification by specializing in Nephrology, and caring for patients with End Stage Renal failure. By the age of 50 Mom had not only achieved her childhood dream career but she had purchased a home and ensured the success of her three children who by then all had careers. I became an educator, author and speaker; my sister is a registered nurse and my brother has his own business as an auto-electrician. At the age of 50 we honoured her publicly for her sacrifice and persistence which has paid off tremendously. Mom continues to work at KPH. However, her academic pursuits are not over. At the age of 52, she wants to further her studies and do her masters in nursing education so that she can become a lecturer. Mom is a member of the Tower Hill Missionary Church where she leads their annual health fair initiative as well as assists with the Senior Citizen's group. Mom wants to be remembered as the lady who never gave up on her dreams. She also does motivational speaking with me. Now, can you see why I am so proud of her? From her story here are three lessons on attitudes that lead to success, for you to reflect on and adopt.

LESSON 31: PERSEVERE AND FAIL FORWARD

Mom did not allow her failures to stop her from achieving her dream and neither should you. Every dream will be tested. You cannot achieve success if you do not persevere. To persevere is to resolve not to give up until you get the right results. To persevere means that we keep trying until we achieve our goal. Only by persevering can we fail forward. The concept of "failing forward" means using failure as fuel to push us further along instead of letting failure serve as a stumbling block. It means having a mindset that failure only means that I need to learn more skills. It means not taking failure as a personal attack on our capability. It means seeing failure as further attempts in learning to get the right results. It means as Les Brown says, "If it is worth doing, then it is worth doing wrong until you get it right." Let my mom's 38 years of chasing her dream push you to achieve yours. Don't ever give up!

LESSON 32: GO THE EXTRA MILE

My mom went the extra mile. She sacrificed for her children in the process and extended herself beyond what was expected, in ways that would ensure their success, while putting her dreams on hold. But even in the pursuit of her dreams she did more than was expected. This is one of the secrets of success. Even at Mom's age, she is willing to go back to school to further develop her skills to achieve more success even though it's not a need. You must be willing to extend yourself if you truly want to succeed. When you are willing to work harder and do more, doors and opportunities will be opened unto you. It's the law of sowing and reaping and the greater the sowing, the greater the measure of reaping. Don't be afraid to go the extra mile.

LESSON 33: BE FLEXIBLE, ADAPTABLE AND TEACHABLE

In the context of working towards your dreams and goals, being flexible and adaptable means openness and willingness to change and make the necessary adjustments along the way. You will discover in the pursuit of your goal or dream that very often you will be required to adjust your timelines, your methodology and your expectations. Things will not always go as planned and sometimes the dream or goal needs refinement, which over time with greater understanding, your goal and strategies may necessitate change. Being teachable means being willing to learn along the journey. Mom tried a number of different things to make ends meet. She gradually increased her skills and value. She had some mis-steps but she learnt lessons along the way. Eventually after many years she was able to take the right steps that led her closer to her dream. She learnt to adapt to her circumstances and deal well with the hand she was dealt. She was teachable and willing to follow good counsel. Our plans will not always go as we expect. There will be setbacks but as long as we are flexible, adaptable and teachable, success will be ours.

IT'S TIME TO INTROSPECT

1. *Is there a dream in your heart that is still worth pursuing?*
2. *Have you experienced failure along the way and feel like giving up? Make a decision today to dream again and persevere despite your adversities and setbacks. It's time to fail forward. If Marva can do it after 38 years of struggle, so can you!*
3. *Determine in your heart that you will grow like a strong tree. Exercise flexibility, adaptability and go the extra mile as you pursue your goals and dreams. It will definitely pay off.*

Where there is a will, you will definitely find a way. Stay tuned for tomorrow's tree talk on personal growth and change

RESPONSE TO TREE TALK

What actions will you take as a result of this tree talk? Or what decisions will you make?

TALK 12
PERSONAL GROWTH
AND CHANGE

We run tings, tings nuh run we.
(We control our destiny.)
[Jamaican Proverb]

IT'S TIME TO CHANGE

"If you don't like your current address, change it. You're not a tree." Yes, you, I'm talking to you. Many of us like to blame the government, our parents, our spouses and a whole host of others for the way things are and for our failure to achieve success, but for things to change you have to change. It was Jim Rohn, the great American, business philosopher who popularized the saying: "For things to change, you have to change. If you don't like your current address, change it. You're not a tree." It is true. If you don't like the way things are, change it. You're not a tree. Today, we will look at three lessons on personal growth and change.

LESSON 34: TAKE FULL RESPONSIBILITY FOR YOUR CHANGE AND GROWTH

A tree cannot move itself. Once planted it can be transplanted but generally it stays put, and adjusts to the changes of life until it dies or is blown down by the winds and storms of life, is cut down or rots. Humans, however, are not like trees. We have choice and a will. If our current environment is not contributing to the positive results we desire, we can change it. If our current education or salary is not at the level we want it to be we can change it. Instead of striking or protesting for higher wages, why not improve your market value and get a better job? But it's easier to blame the government, our upbringing and the injustices that have happened to us rather than take personal responsibility for our lives and the state we are in.

I believe once we reach adulthood we are responsible for our actions. We must take personal responsibility for our attitude and responses to things. Change very often will not come unless we decide to change and take action. "If you don't like the way things are, change it. You're not a tree... For things to change, you have to change."

LESSON 35: INVEST IN YOURSELF; INCREASE YOUR VALUE IF YOU WANT TO HAVE MORE

Another Jim Rohn saying is this: "work harder on yourself than you do on your job. The greatest investment is in yourself." It is as you grow personally that you will become more useful and valuable to the market place and the greater your reward will be. My mom took the time to invest in herself, to become more and thus she was able to improve her lot in life and escape poverty. When you increase your value, opportunities will abound. Even if you lose a job, you will never lose your value and that value can be used elsewhere when one door closes.

The difference between the person earning minimum wage and the Chief Executive Officer is in personal growth and value to the market place. If the person earning minimum wage increases his/her value by learning more and increasing his/her skills, one day that person can own the company. It will take time but it's a story that's been told before. It is a story I love to hear, from being the janitor or waitress to becoming the company owner. So my friend, create your personal growth plan today. The investment in yourself over time will yield great rewards. Read all the books you can, ask all the questions you can, hone your skills, practice to become outstanding at what you do and slowly but surely the rewards will come.

LESSON 36: MAKE ADJUSTMENTS FOR MAXIMUM GROWTH

Have you ever seen a tree swaying in the wind? Have you ever seen a tree bending towards the direction of the sunlight? The tree is making adjustments to grow and flourish because it cannot change its address. Trees bend, sink their roots deeper and take nourishment from the soil to fuel their growth and development so that they can grow to their full height. Evergreen trees are masters at adjusting or adapting to their environment for maximum growth. They thrive no matter the climate. I'll share more on these later in the book but the point is: trees adjust to reach their goal of ultimate growth. Their desire to grow is unquenchable, unwavering and often unstoppable. Set your mind on what you want to accomplish. It's not the circumstances of life that determine where you end up, it's your commitment to arrive at your intended destination that determines your success. Like trees, we often have no control over the people and situations around us, and while we may not be able to change the environment, we can change ourselves, our attitudes and our behaviour. We can make the necessary adjustments to the people and situations around us for our ultimate growth and success.

IT'S TIME TO INTROSPECT

1. *How deep is your desire to grow personally?*
2. *What adjustments are you willing to make to achieve these goals and attain personal success?*
3. *Are you giving yourself sufficient time to grow?*

Where there is a will, you will definitely find a way. Stay tuned for tomorrow's tree talk on your masterplan and internal design for growth and productivity.

RESPONSE TO TREE TALK

What actions will you take as a result of this tree talk? Or what decisions will you make?

TALK 13
YOUR MASTER PLAN AND INTERNAL DESIGN

If you bawn fi heng, yu cyaa drown.
(Your destiny will be fulfilled.)
[Jamaican Proverb]

WHERE IS YOUR BLUEPRINT?

Trees seem to have an inbuilt design for growth and an inbuilt master plan for bearing fruit. Seeds have an inbuilt vision, plan and timelines for growth and reproduction. Seeds know just how long to stay in the soil, when to emerge from the soil, when to shoot, when to flower, when to reproduce and when to die. They grow at their own pace. Fruit trees in particular grow to full height and repeatedly bear fruit in abundance at particular times and seasons. These trees also ensure their survival for successive generations through the new seeds and fruits produced annually.

Nevertheless, despite these plans, we know that many things can hinder or stifle the growth of a fruit tree and sometimes a fruit tree may grow but produce no fruit. There are often distortions and diseases which inhibit and hinder the tree's functionality. However in this talk, I would like to focus not so much on the distortions but on the inbuilt design and capacity to grow and bear fruit and the lessons we can learn from the trees in this regard.

LESSON 37: TREES HAVE A VISION AND PLAN (BLUEPRINT) AND SO SHOULD YOU

The trees know their purpose. Seeds see the end from the beginning and once planted grow towards it unlike many humans who seem to be merely existing. I believe the clues to our design are wrapped up in our gifts, likes, interests and what we are good at or drawn to. Not all of us can sing like Celine Dion or run like Usain Bolt but we all can do something and achieve some degree of success in that something. Sometimes it calls for a little experimentation before we fully recognize what our design truly is, that is, before we recognize what we have been created to do and how we should do it. Sometimes it calls for the right relationships because relationships determine our destiny.

If we do not know what our design is, it's time to ask the Great Intelligent Designer of the universe, our Creator, to reveal it to us. When we ask, ideas usually come to mind and sometimes supernatural things happen. Sometimes the Great Designer sends someone our way, who recognizes our gifts and sees the vision of what we could become who helps us along the way. For example, it was Usain Bolt's father who saw his potential as an athlete and encouraged him to follow that path. It was someone who saw Denzel Washington's potential as an actor and told him to pursue that path when he did not know what to do with his life and was flunking out of college. Sometimes the helpers are actual talent scouts and coaches who have the ability to see and develop a gift for maximum effect.

Without vision a people will perish. Without a well designed plan, your destination will be uncertain. If you don't know where you are going, any road will take you there. If trees, which are less valuable than humans, have a well designed plan for growth and development, how much more should we as humans? Jim Rohn once challenged his audience with the following words: "Five years from now you will certainly arrive, the question is where? You will either arrive at a well designed destination or an un-designed destination. Wouldn't it be better to arrive at a well-designed destination?" These words are my challenge to you as well.

LESSON 38: KNOW YOUR SEASON AND FUNCTION ACCORDING TO YOUR DESIGN

A mango tree is not a banana tree. A soursop does not produce mangoes and a banana tree does not produce avocadoes. Function according to your design and function according to your timetable and season. As mentioned before, all the fruit trees in my backyard do not bear at the same time nor do they all grow at the same pace. Some are taller than others and some bear more fruit than others. I do not expect the soursop tree to produce yields like the mango tree and neither is it competing with the mango tree. Each tree follows its own design. With this in mind we should have less frustration and anxiety in the pursuit of personal success.

Recently my friend, Kenyatta, reminded me of something important about trees that grow in colder climates. These trees, in winter, may appear dead to a person like me from the tropics. They have no leaves. They make no food and are not great to look at. These trees go through a process of dormancy which is like the hibernation of bears. Growth is stalled and impeded to save energy during winter. This process ensures their survival and come spring, leaves begin to grow on these same trees. They begin to flower and then come alive again. Sometimes we get frustrated because we are not flowering like others but could it be that it is not our time to flower? You need to function according to your design and in your season. Life may look like winter but hey, your spring will come!

LESSON 39: YOU ARE DESIGNED TO BE A FRUITFUL HUMAN BEING

Why should you be given talents and abilities and do nothing with them? What good is a car that cannot be driven or a cell phone that does not work? Genesis 1: 26-28 reveals the Great Designer's plan for human beings:

> Then God said, "Let us make human beings in our image and likeness. And let them rule over the fish in the sea and the birds in the sky, over the tame animals, over all the earth, and over all the small crawling animals on the earth." So God created human beings in his image. In the image of God he created them. He created them male and female. God blessed them and said, "Have many children and grow in number. Fill the earth and be its master. Rule over the fish in the sea and over the birds in the sky and over every living thing that moves on the earth.

Human beings are created with a purpose and commanded to be fruitful. To be fruitful means to be productive and producing positive results. We are expected to use our gifts and talents to produce positive results. We should manage the earth's resources well and produce positive results. We are expected to produce multiple yields in our endeavours, to increase our value and not just our number in terms of offspring. Do not just write one book, write many books, produce many songs, produce many good things and manage them well. Fruitfulness or maximum productivity in all good things should be our aim. Are you living a fruitful life or are you like the cursed fig tree in Mark 11? Are you merely existing and occupying space?

It's Time to Introspect

1. *Do you have a vision and plan for your life?*
2. *Do you know your purpose and the contribution you should make while you are here on earth?*
3. *What season are you in on your journey to success?*
4. *Do you really believe that you were designed to be fruitful?*

Where there is a will, you will definitely find a way. Stay tuned for tomorrow's tree talk about producing your own kind and celebrating your special brand.

Response to Tree Talk

What actions will you take as a result of this tree talk? Or what decisions will you make?

TALK 14
YOUR OWN KIND:
YOUR SPECIAL BRAND

If yu see everybody a run tek time.
(Don't be too eager to follow others.)
[Jamaican Proverb]

BEING TRULY UNIQUE

It is often said that variety is the spice of life. There is no one type of animals, no one type of phones, no one type of cars, houses or trees. Trees come in different shapes and sizes. There are several types of trees or tree species in the world. These act as a habitat for over 140,000 animal species and other micro-organisms.[8] In the same way human beings are unique. No one else has our DNA or finger prints. Indeed diversity pervades our universe and as such we need not strive to live like everyone else. Our uniqueness should be celebrated. This means we should each seek to follow our unique paths even if we are in the same field. There is a Jamaican proverb that reflects this truth: "Every hoe has its stick a bush."

When diversity and variety are not celebrated, we have pride, racism, classism, disunity, jealousy and all the ills that follow. In the tree kingdom, the trees are not competing with each other but each develops and bears its own kind of fruit based on its inbuilt design. In my backyard each of the seven trees occupies its own space and is not competing even though they all exist in the same backyard, planted in the same soil, needing the same essential ingredients for growth (air, soil, sunlight and water). Imagine if we as humans could pattern the trees in my backyard, how beautiful would our world be! If trees can do it, why not us? O the wisdom of the trees!

LESSON 40: PRODUCE AFTER YOUR KIND; FIND YOUR NICHE

If you were a tree what kind would you be? Know your identity. Study your tree. Plant your tree. Bear your fruit. You never see a mango tree producing lime or a lime tree producing oranges. Each produces after its own kind. Stop trying to be like everyone else. Even within the same field there is variety. Become leader not a follower and stamp your own brand even in a common field. Are there not varieties of mangoes, bananas, limes and avocados? Therefore, discover your uniqueness. Become more self aware and understand yourself. Produce after your kind. Find your niche and create your own brand. Develop your brand. Become an expert in your field and maximize your potential.

LESSON 41: THERE IS A MARKET FOR YOUR NICHE AND YOUR BRAND

Not everyone loves mangoes. Some people do not even eat mangoes as delicious as they are. Some prefer apples and soursop. For varying reasons people have different tastes and appetites. That's just how things are on this planet. In my conversation with the trees, the trees said to me: "There will always be a market for your products. Do not fret about the abundance of trees and in my case, the fact that there are so many books on the market." In the same way we have our preference for fruits, so will I have my set of followers, clients and consumers. There will always be market for your harvest, that is, for your brand. Your gift will make room for you. Don't worry about a glut on the market. "Every hoe has its stick a bush."

This truth is demonstrable in the life of Nick Vuijic. I remember years ago when Nick Vuijic, the man who has no arms and legs, said he believed one day he would marry. This seemed farfetched to me given the magnitude of his disability. However in 2012, Nick Vuijic married a beautiful able-bodied woman and today they have a son and are in ministry. She chose him over many able-bodied men.[9] I am sure Nick's beautiful, ambitious heart, purpose and mind played a role. We are more than our bodies and certainly there is a place and market for each of us. Seek to find it or create it. There is a market for your niche and brand.

LESSON 42: CELEBRATE YOUR UNIQUENESS

I love to show off the trees in my backyard especially when the harvest is great. I love the fact that we have varieties. Each tree imparts a different lesson, serves a specific purpose and meets a specific need. In the same way each of us has been designed for a specific purpose and to meet a specific need. For this reason we should celebrate our uniqueness. There is no one else like you, no other with your finger print or DNA. If you don't appreciate or celebrate your uniqueness, it is difficult for others to do so. The more we celebrate our uniqueness, the more we will also appreciate the uniqueness of others. Don't be a mango tree envying the cherry tree! There is enough space or room for everyone. Since there is a place for your gifts and abilities, there will be a place where these will also be celebrated.

IT'S TIME TO INTROSPECT

1. Who are you competing with or jealous of?
2. Who are you comparing yourself to?
3. Have you discovered your niche?
4. Are you celebrating your uniqueness?

Where there is a will, you will definitely find a way. Stay tuned for tomorrow's tree talk on managing your growth and development

RESPONSE TO TREE TALK

What actions will you take as a result of this tree talk? Or what decisions will you make?

TALK 15
MANAGING YOUR GROWTH AND DEVELOPMENT

Sick nu care, doctor worst.
(If you don't care about your
own problems, don't expect
anyone else to care.)
[Jamaican Proverb]

MY NEIGHBOUR'S MANGO TREES

Over a year ago, our neighbour, much to my land-lady's delight cut the large limbs and branches of two of his mango trees which were encroaching on my landlady's property. While this meant less work for us, it also meant less of those lovely East Indian and Blackie mangoes which were not in our back-yard. But now some of the branches have re-grown and I am once again enjoying two of my favourite kinds of mangoes. Nevertheless, as much as I am enjoying the fruits, I know that cutting time is not far away and whether I like it or not, it must be done. When trees are in our backyards their growth must be guided, guarded and managed well. These trees need to be monitored and properly cared for if our backyards are going to remain clean, safe and pleasing to the eyes. It is the same with our growth and development and here are three lessons in this regard.

LESSON 43: MONITOR YOUR GROWTH AND DEVELOPMENT

Monitoring the growth of trees in your backyard is very important, especially when you live on a hurricane prone tropical island. It is also of utmost importance to carefully consider where you plant the tree. I wonder how many persons have lost their roofs or have had their roofs damaged in a hurricane because of overgrown trees and branches and limbs which grew too close to the house? How many times have we seen men from the electric power company come to cut tree limbs which have grown too close to the electric wires? If those trees are not cut, harm will come to someone. In the same way we need to monitor our growth and personal development. We need to monitor our physical health and monitor the growth of our families, companies, ministries and whatever else we have been given to manage.

We need to know when it is time to cut expenditure or to cut something that is harmful or getting out of control. This means monitoring our habits and thought life and our associations. It means monitoring our finances and seeing if our finances are growing out of control or growing well. It means continually revisiting our goals to see if we on target and to see if we are fulfilling our mission and vision. Are you monitoring your growth wholistically? Are you growing spiritually and emotionally? Are you lopsided? What area of your life has been left neglected and unchecked and is now growing out of control?

LESSON 44: BE ON GUARD AGAINST DISEASE, DECAY AND DEATH

The lime tree and the pear tree in my backyard are no longer producing great yields. The storms and hurricanes have greatly affected their levels of production. Some of the mango trees have become diseased. Sometimes the mangoes are filled with worms and black spots and are not edible. The drought has affected the soursop as well. The soursop trees appear to be dying. Disease, decay and death are all part of life and at some stage we will experience all three. However, there are cases in which all three are preventable or significantly delayed based on how we manage ourselves. Some diseases are caused by failure to monitor what we eat; becoming obese, hypertensive or diabetic. Proper dieting and exercise greatly aid in treating and preventing some disease and decay and help us to live happier, healthier and longer.

We must guard not only against physical diseases but diseases of attitude like indifference, indecision, ingratitude, doubt, fear, worry, pessimism and complaint. We must also guard against mental decay by aiming to be lifelong learners. This is one of the ingredients of success. We should read or listen to something uplifting and enlightening at least 15 minutes each day. As our knowledge increases so does our value and the opportunities to increase our earnings and contribution to society. Don't let the storms and adversities of life kill your dream, kill your spirit or destroy your life. Fight against disease, decay and death as long as you are breathing.

LESSON 45: BEWARE OF THIEVES AND TAKE PROTECTIVE ACTION

There are those who love to reap where they have not sown. We in Jamaica know that ever so often there are those who will raid our fruit trees and go to the market to sell our fruits without giving us the owners a dime. There are those who through scamming will steal your hard earned money. We have been made aware for several years now of the lottery scam that has been associated with my beloved country much to my shame. Nevertheless, as much as many of us are aware of the external thieves, not many of us are aware of the internal thieves in our mind and hearts such as fear and doubt which also rob us of our fruit and productivity.

Fear immobilizes and cripples us so that we cannot seize the opportunities around us. It causes talents to be buried and unused and sometimes we die without releasing it. Fear of rejection, fear of death, fear of loss of love, fear of becoming old and fear of failure are major thieves which need to be arrested and locked up behind bars for good with no possibility of parole. We must daily fight against these internal thieves by renewing our minds and developing winning habits. We must believe that we can overcome them. They must be made subject to the laws of success. Unless we take protective action, these thieves will continue to rob us of the fruitful life our Divine Designer intended for us to enjoy.

It's Time to Introspect

1. *Are you monitoring your growth?*
2. *Are you guarding against disease, decay and death?*
3. *Are you aware of the thieves that are out to rob you of success?*
4. *What protective actions will you take?*

Where there is a will, you will definitely find a way. Stay tuned for tomorrow's tree talk on the price of fruitfulness.

Response to Tree Talk

What actions will you take as a result of this tree talk? Or what decisions will you make?

TALK 16
THE PRICE OF
FRUITFULNESS

If yu waa good, yu nose affi run.
(Success requires hard work.)
[Jamaican Proverb]

A TIME TO EAT AND
A TIME TO SWEEP

It's now the end of the mango season and oh my we have our work cut out for us! The tree is shedding leaves like crazy and we need to sweep twice per day or risk seeing the yard looking rather unsightly with dry leaves. As much as I love mangoes, I really do not like this part, the constant cleaning. It was also the same thing during the harvest season. We had to be constantly picking up and distributing mangoes because too many mangoes on the ground means pests and rodents like rats and flies. It also grieves me to see things wasted. Being fruitful comes with a price but as Jim Rohn rightly said, "if you know the prize, you will pay the price." Cleaning and collection are but small prices to pay for the joys and benefits of fruitfulness. Now let's look at today's three lessons on the price of fruitfulness.

LESSON 46: PAY THE
PRICE TO BE FRUITFUL

"The heights by great men reached and kept were not attained by sudden flight but they while their companions slept were toiling upwards through the night." The price for success must be paid in full. Shelly-Ann Fraser-Pryce, the world's fastest woman cannot neglect training if she expects to win gold medals and remain the fastest woman in the world, and neither can you neglect personal development and discipline, if you intend to be successful and fruitful. We must choose our suffering, either the price of regret or the price of discipline. Rohn, the great wordsmith, notes: "The price of discipline weighs ounces; the price of regret weighs tonnes."

If the farmer eats the entire crop, there will be no harvest next season. He has to save seeds to plant no matter how much his family desires to eat it. When we apply this principle to life in general there are significant lessons. This may mean living where we do not want to live temporarily so that in the long run we can have our dream home. This may mean less time socializing with friends; less time spent being on social media and watching TV, so that we can study in order to improve our skills for greater financial rewards and improvement in our standard of living. In a word, paying the price to be fruitful, means "discipline." It is making yourself do what you need to do whether you feel like it or not, so that you can reap the long term rewards. It is short-term pain for long term gain. Resolve to pay the price to be fruitful today and if the promise of the future is clear, it is definitely easier to pay the price.

LESSON 47: PAY ATTENTION TO THE TREE, NOT JUST THE FRUITS

During mango season, we often get more visitors than normal. The tasty fruit attracts all kinds of people. These people for the most part are only interested in the fruit. They are not necessarily interested in the owner of the tree or the tree itself, just the fruits. Nevertheless, without the owner there would have been no tree and without the tree, there would be no fruits for passersby to enjoy. This scenario in itself can teach us many life lessons.

For example: have you ever wondered why sometimes many stars and many of the wealthy and famous turn to drugs and some commit suicide? Could it be that that they really have few friends or people who genuinely care about them because the people around them are only interested in the fruit and not the tree? This would certainly lead to despair. When attention is only paid to the fruit, this is dangerous because sooner or later there will be no fruit if the tree is neglected.

Those who enjoy the fruit often do not see the tending that takes place. Sometimes we even have to cut the tree to make it more fruitful. Sometimes the tree has to be fertilized. As an individual, you are the tree that bears the fruit. You should keep sharpening your skills and take good care of yourself and the gifts you have been given. You must care for your body, soul and mind or else your fruitfulness will be cut short. Know when to rest and get adequate sleep. You also pay attention to your "tree" by maintaining your connection with your Divine Designer through daily times of prayer and meditation. Remember you are not just a body but a spirit.

You need to nourish your mind by reading more in your field, by reading inspirational material and by listening to daily motivational messages. Whatsoever things are pure, honest, praiseworthy and of good report; think on these things (Philippians 4:8). We must pay attention to our thought life and be careful of what we permit to enter our minds. We do become what we think about and as a man thinks in his heart, so is he. Since our lives follow our thoughts, we should invest in listening to valuable material to counter the negative thoughts in our heads and those that come from our environment. Listening to inspirational material while travelling is a wonderful way to save time and get your daily nourishment. Do this instead of always listening to music or things that are unhelpful in relation to your goals. Paying attention to these things will preserve your tree and result in ongoing fruitfulness.

LESSON 48: DON'T BECOME TOO PREOCCUPIED WITH FRUITFULNESS

Have you ever heard of someone on their death bed wishing they had spent more time at the office? Sometimes we are so busy bearing fruit and seeking success that in the end we lose the things that really matter. I have heard it said that as much as 80% of our happiness is connected to our relationships. Many times we chase material things to the detriment of our health, our relationships and our peace of mind. Thus one may eventually get the dream home but live in it alone, estranged from spouse and children. As Mali Music puts it: "At the end of the day, it's no fun being alone." Nobody really wants to be alone. Get the material things which come with fruitfulness but do not neglect the things that fruitfulness cannot buy.

Don't become a fruitful fool. The Lord Jesus reminds us that it does not profit to gain the whole world and lose your soul (Mark 8:36). A man's life is not measured in the abundance of his possessions (Luke 4:15) and we should guard against all kinds of greed. Life is more than food and clothes or material things.

IT'S TIME TO INTROSPECT

1. *Will you pay the full price for fruitfulness?*
2. *Are you neglecting your tree and only focussing on the fruit?*
3. *Have you become too preoccupied with productivity to the detriment of your relationships or the things that really matter?*

Where there is a will, you will definitely find a way. Stay tuned for tomorrow's tree talk about being fruitfully responsible.

RESPONSE TO TREE TALK

What actions will you take as a result of this tree talk? Or what decisions will you make?

TALK 17
BEING FRUITFULLY
RESPONSIBLE

Di house whe shelta yu when a rain,
look fi it when sun hot.
(When you become successful, look
out for those who helped you during
your hard times.)
[Jamaican Proverb]

SOCIAL ENTREPRENEURS

In 2014, I became aware of a concept that totally intrigued me because it reflected a goal I have had for a long time and a key part of my mission in life. It was the concept of being a "Social Entrepreneur." According to the Skoll World Forum, **social entrepreneurs** pave avenues of opportunity for those who would, otherwise, be locked into lives without hope. Social entrepreneurs are society's change agents, creators of innovations that disrupt the status quo and transform our world.

Social entrepreneurs are ambitious, mission driven, strategic, resourceful and results oriented. They tackle major social issues, from increasing the college enrolment rate of low-income students to fighting poverty. They operate in all kinds of organizations: innovative non-profits, social-purpose ventures, and hybrid organizations that mix elements of non-profit and for-profit organizations. Generating social value—not wealth—is the central criterion of a successful social entrepreneur. While wealth creation may be part of the process, it is not an end in itself. Promoting systemic social change is the real objective.

Like business entrepreneurs, social entrepreneurs see and act upon what others miss: opportunities to improve systems, create solutions and invent new approaches that create social value. Like the best business entrepreneurs, social entrepreneurs are intensely focused and hard-driving in their pursuit of a social vision. Social entrepreneurs are driven to produce measurable returns. These results transform existing realities, open up new pathways for the marginalized and disadvantaged, and unlock society's potential to effect social change.[10]

There is a correlation with trees and social entrepreneurship. Trees do not only produce food for themselves but food for humans and animals alike. Trees create social value and are indispensable to our survival. They provide shade and homes for animals and humans alike. We should seek to emulate the tree in this regard. When we become successful and begin to bear fruit in abundance, year after year, like trees, we must use our fruitfulness to build our society and to build the lives of others. Those with much material goods should help those without. The haves bear a responsibility to help the have nots. To whom much is given, much is required because we are and ought to be our brother's keeper. Today we will look at three instructions to live by in order to bear fruit responsibly, to be fruitfully responsible and be our brother's keeper.

LESSON 49: REMEMBER THE TRUE SOURCE OF THE FRUIT

None of the trees in my backyard planted themselves and although my landlady planted several of them, she did not create the trees or the seed. The trees did not create the soil, water, sunlight and nutrients they need to grow and produce fruit. As humans, we often fail to attribute our accomplishments to our Divine Designer and Creator. Some of us think it's our mere intellect and effort that have enabled us to be successful but this not true. Each of us was given the gift of this body and the gift of resources on earth to utilize for the benefit of all. You did not make this body with a brain, internal and external organs and a mind. You did not create the air to breathe or the earth to live on. Furthermore, all of these things can also be taken from us in a moment's notice via death, sickness or disaster. The one who is wealthy today could be poor tomorrow. The one who has abundance today could be in need tomorrow.

The story of King Nebuchadnezzar, the great king of Babylon and ruler over many kingdoms, should be a warning to us all. He was like a tree on earth that grew to a great height and became strong. Its height reached to the heavens and could be seen all over the earth. Its leaves were lovely, its fruit abundant and in it was food for all. The beasts of the field found shade under it, the birds of the heavens dwelt in its branches and all flesh was fed from it. But then a holy one from heaven decreed:

Cut down the tree and cut off its branches. Strip off its leaves and scatter its fruit. Let the animals under the tree run away, and let the birds in its branches fly away. But leave the stump and its roots in the ground with a band of iron and bronze around it; let it stay in the field with the grass around it. "'Let the man become wet with dew, and let him live among the animals and plants of the earth. Let him not think like a human any longer, but let him have the mind of an animal for seven years. 'The observers gave this command; the holy ones declared the sentence. This is so all people may know that the Most High God rules over every kingdom on earth. God gives those kingdoms to anyone he wants, and he chooses people to rule them who are not proud."(Daniel 4:10-17)

Nebuchadnezzar was proud. He attributed all his success to himself. Pride always go before a fall. Nebuchadnezzar became insane for a while until he learnt the valuable lesson that he was not self-made and should credit his success to the Creator and Divine Designer of the universe.

LESSON 50: REMEMBER THE PURPOSE OF THE FRUIT

What is the purpose of a fruit? Is it merely for food consumption or to keep us healthy? The primary function of a fruit is for reproduction to perpetuate plant species. Fruits protect the seeds.[11] Trees produce fruits to nourish and protect the seeds. If something does not eat the fruit, it falls to the ground, decays and fertilizes the soil where the seed will grow to produce a tree. In likc manner, if we think of our fruitfulness as a means to preserve our species, then we would be more willing to share our successes and our resources. When the purpose of a thing is misunderstood, abuse takes place or it is misused. Fruitfulness should not be merely for our individual benefit or our family's benefit. We are to be our brother's keeper. We should seek to help others like social entrepreneurs.

We need more people like Usain Bolt and Shelly-Ann Fraser-Pryce who use their success to give back to those who are less fortunate and to build their communities. Usain Bolt has invested some of his resources to enhance programmes at his former High school, William Knibb. Shelly-Ann Fraser-Pryce has a foundation to help high school students. Bill and Melinda Gates and a number of other successful people also have foundations and are actively giving back. Now it could be argued that more can be done but the point is as we chart our own journey to success, we should make giving back a non-negotiable goal.

LESSON 51: REMEMBER TO TEACH OTHERS HOW TO BE FRUITFUL

Fruits contain seeds and when that seed is planted, it will grow to become trees which will produce more fruit. Our aim should not be to only become fruitful but to teach others to be fruitful. We should pass on the seeds of success and sow into the lives of others so they too can be fruitful. It is not enough to just share your material resources when you become successful, show others how to be successful. This is one of the reasons I write to show others how they too can overcome their situations; to give them the tools and ideas that have changed my life so that their lives can also be changed. This is what Extra MILE Innovators is all about, creating initiatives to motivate, inspire, liberate and empower others to be successful and live the meaningful lives they were designed to live. When we teach others to be fruitful, this is truly being fruitfully responsible.

IT'S TIME TO INTROSPECT

1. *In what way are you being your brother's keeper?*
2. *Are you bearing fruit responsibly?*
3. *Are you investing any of your resources (your fruit) in the lives of others?*
4. *Have you recognized or remembered the true source of your success?*

Where there is a will, you will definitely find a way. Stay tuned for tomorrow's tree talk on securing your financial harvest.

RESPONSE TO TREE TALK

What actions will you take as a result of this tree talk? Or what decisions will you make?

TALK 18
SECURING YOUR
FINANCIAL HARVEST

Nyam some, lef some.
(Plan for tomorrow; Don't consume
everything all at once.)
[Jamaican Proverb]

THE RAINY DAY PLAN

Many of us struggle from pay check to pay check. We do not have that 3-8 month's salary saving buffer that our financial institutions encourage us to have. Most of us are two pay cheques from being home-less. We have no rainy day savings, nothing set aside for a natural disaster, for famine, hurricane or drought, sickness or children's education, but if we plant like trees we will always have something even in times of disaster, be it man made or natural.

I remember my first hurricane, the 1988 hurricane Gilbert. I was 8 years old and living in St Mary with my grandmother. We virtually lost our home in that disaster. We were praying and singing a hymn when the roof went. But prior to losing the roof to the wind, as it rained, I vividly remember us watching the pear (avocado) tree. It was pear season and as the wind blew, and the pears fell, we the children, would run outside in the wind and rain to pick up pears. It was great fun for us! After the hurricane had passed for days our main food was breadfruit and pear. There was breadfruit in abundance.

You see, despite the disaster, the trees we planted had borne fruit and we had supply amidst this disaster. It is important to plant our financial trees in the same way. If we plant a tree even when there is job loss, slow market, we can survive or recover quickly in the face of adversities. We will also never run out of supply. What's your tree or seed? What trees will you plant to ensure supply even in times of economic disaster? What trees will you plant to move past being just over broke? What trees will you plant for future critical needs? Let us now proceed to today's three lessons on securing a financial harvest.

LESSON 52: PLANT TREES TO SECURE A FINANCIAL HARVEST FOR YOURSELF AND OTHERS

In my backyard, there are seven trees which I never planted, and yet, for the past five years I have benefitted from them. The moringa tree has brought tremendous health benefits; the mango trees have been a constant fill in times where food was scarce; the lime trees have enabled me to refresh my house guests with delicious drinks and the same could be said of the soursop tree. My landlady said she knew one day they would come in handy and that's why she planted them. I bet she never imagined just how handy they would become to me! In a similar way we should utilize our gifts in a way that others will continue to benefit in the future. For example, with my gift of writing I can write books and benefit monetarily from them long after publication. This financial benefit may very well extend to my children and grandchildren as a result of my one -time effort in this season. What is it that you will develop through a one-time effort that will yield ongoing financial rewards? What's your tree? Will you plant a tree today? What kind of tree will you plant? How will you ensure it produces a harvest more than adequate for yourself and others?

LESSON 53: PLANT DIFFERENT KINDS OF TREES SO THAT THEY WILL PRODUCE FRUIT AT DIFFERENT SEASONS

All the trees in my backyard do not bear fruit at the same time or season. Imagine if a farmer is only depending on one crop or type of tree? He would sure go hungry at some stage. We need to diversify or have multiple income streams. Therefore plant different trees so there will always be fruit, that is, there will always be an income flow. Remember in our storm we had both breadfruit and pear to make a delicious meal. Therefore, what are the other means of income that can be derived while you wait on a particular tree to grow and bear fruit? In my case I am not only an author, but a trained teacher and a speaker so while I write books, I could teach and speak, so that there will always be an income flow. These are my trees and I can later specialize by mass producing one particular kind of tree for the long term.

LESSON 54: PLAN PROPERLY FOR YOUR FINANCIAL HARVEST

I remember when our mango trees produced so many Julie mangoes that we had a hard time trying to give them all away. Many were spoiled and thrown in the garbage because we did not prepare properly for the harvest. How many times have you heard of superstars going broke after earning millions? How many times have lottery winners returned to poverty? If you fail to prepare for the harvest, you will waste it. If you get a million dollars and do not have a million dollar mind, you will lose it quickly. Are you only planting trees or are you also preparing for the harvest? Are you only developing your skill or are you also preparing for success? The time to start preparing is before you start planting. Remember prior, proper, planning prevents poor performance. Thankfully, it is never too late to go in the right direction...better late than never.

Indeed the trees were telling me to start preparing for my future financial harvest. My books will one day produce great yields as the trees in my backyard. A book is very much like a tree. Once written and published it can be reprinted and sold over and over again, much like a tree producing fruit year after year. If however, I am not prepared for the harvest, the yields may be wasted and it could be as if I never planted a tree and I could end up five years from now crying over my pitiful finances. You see, we not only reap what we sow, we reap more than we sow.

Therefore envision the harvest and plan now for it before it comes. For example, if we expect a plentiful harvest, we must now make a list of all the labourers needed, all the equipment needed, the different ways to sell and market the crop a well as methods for collecting payment, so that when the harvest comes we will not be ill-prepared. We must properly prepare for the multiplied yields.

IT'S TIME TO INTROSPECT

1. *Are you securing your financial harvest?*
2. *Are you seeking abundance so that you can contribute to others as well as yourself?*
3. *What plans do you have in place for the financial harvest that is coming your way?*
4. *How will you ensure that the harvest is not wasted?*
5. *What tree will you plant today for future financial fruitfulness?*

Where there is a will, you will definitely find a way. Stay tuned for tomorrow's tree talk on production and monetization.

RESPONSE TO TREE TALK

What actions will you take as a result of this tree talk? Or what decisions will you make?

TALK 19
PRODUCTION AND MONETIZATION

Daag seh im won't work. Im wi siddung an look, fah im mus get a libin.
(Some people prefer to wait on others to give them handouts instead of working for their own money)
[Jamaican Proverb]

USE YOUR MIND

Too many of us want to enjoy the harvest without toiling. We want the easy life or we produce just enough to make ends meet. Fruit trees don't just produce enough fruits, they produce fruits in abundance and we have the ability to do it too. Our Creator has given us the best resource to produce abundantly and reap great rewards. This resource exists between our ears. It is our minds that will enable us to find ways to monetize what we love so that we can care for ourselves and others. This leads us to our three lessons for today.

LESSON 55: PRODUCE LIKE TREES; PRODUCE MORE THAN YOU NEED

Fruit trees always produce abundantly. They mass produce. One mango seed, one lime seed, one pear (avocado) seed produces a tree which yields hundreds of fruit and seeds, year after year if it is not destroyed. This then becomes food and sustenance to the birds of the air and us humans, often leading to health and financial provision and wealth via the creation of secondary tree products, be they food, furniture, paper, cosmetic products, homes etc. This should be our aim in life, not just to produce enough to support ourselves and our family but to support the needs of others. We should produce abundantly, that is, more than enough to enhance our lives and the lives of others.

LESSON 56: MONETIZE YOUR TREE

Whoever said, "money does not grow on trees," perhaps never owned an orchard or never saw the furniture in the trees or the medicine in the trees. Those who own the furniture companies, paper companies and the lumber companies all see the money and now have the wealth to prove it. Those with vision, knowledge and understanding are able to monetize trees. How will you monetize the gift or skill that you have? How will you monetize your ideas, your dreams or inventions? What about your experiences and natural ability? What ideas will you produce which will cause you to earn like trees? How will you monetize your trees? What will you produce to yield multiple streams of income?

LESSON 57: PRODUCE MULTIPLE SEED-LIKE IDEAS FOR MULTIPLE AND ONGOING STREAMS OF INCOME

One good idea can turn you into a millionaire and build a fortune. If ideas are like seeds and we use our imagination, it is possible that we can earn/bear fruit like trees. My visit to the Bob Marley museum in Kingston Jamaica confirmed this idea. I was impressed by the way Bob Marley's music albums (his produce, the fruit of his labour) continue to yield income and how his children continue to benefit from the fruit of his labor so many years after his death. The products (albums) have yielded other ideas which are now yielding millions, even the museum is a spin off, a secondary fruit of his music and his investment in writing and recording his music and albums. If we see ideas like trees, what ideas and products can you give birth to and implement which will reproduce or multiply like trees?

How can we get these ideas? Where does the ability to produce seeds (wealth generating ideas) come from? Who gives the ability to get wealth? Deuteronomy 8:18, "But remember the LORD your **God**, for it is he who **gives** you the **ability to produce wealth**..." Will you ask him to give you that ability today? Furthermore, success teachers encourage us to take at least 20 minutes to one hour in solitude each day to write down 5- 20 ideas in relation to our goals or special projects. Even though, most of these ideas we generate may be no good or worth pursuing, only one good idea is needed. One good idea may become a diamond mine.

IT'S TIME TO INTROSPECT

1. *What is your money tree and how will you monetize it?*
2. *How can you mass produce your products?*
3. *How will you secure ongoing streams of income?*
4. *Are you spending the time daily to generate seed like ideas for your success?*

Where there is a will, you will definitely find a way. Stay tuned for tomorrow's tree talk on accessing and receiving resource.

RESPONSE TO TREE TALK

What actions will you take as a result of this tree talk? Or what decisions will you make?

TALK 20
FINANCIAL
WELL-BEING

Beg wata cyan boil cow kin.
(You can't beg enough water to
boil cow skin, so you need to
look for some yourself.)
[Jamaican Proverb]

I have struggled financially for most of my working life and I believe a large part of that has to do with my beliefs about money and how I spend money. Therefore, if you are struggling financially, you are not alone. In fact, half of the world lives on less than US$2.00 per day and as you recall I began this book with that very dilemma. Nevertheless, do you know anyone who is not struggling financially or always seem to be on top of their finances and has money readily available to help in times of need? Well I know at least one such person: my mom. My mom is like the starfruit always bearing fruit all year round. Like trees she produces abundantly for others to enjoy. She has used her tree (nursing career) to produce fruit that has fed and sustained not just herself but her family and those in her community.

Over the past year, I have been studying her carefully and analyzing her life. She is a nurse who is financially stable and yet I know others who are more qualified than her, who even earn more than she does, and yet they are not financially independent or stable. Since a key principle of success is to study successful persons, I have been studying persons who are doing well financially and I have discovered some principles which I began adopting and I started seeing positive results. I know five years from now things will be radically different financially as a result of applying these principles. Here now are three lessons on becoming financially healthy which I believe we all need to practise as we strive for success.

LESSON 58: SPEND LESS THAN YOU EARN AND SAVE BEFORE SPENDING

The most basic principle of financial well-being is to spend less than you earn and pay yourself first. It is simple but few of us practice it and when income increases we usually increase our spending to match it. The rich actually save and invest first before spending. If we spend all we earn, we will never be financially well. Now you have to make a decision and try to find ways to do it. It may mean eating out less or not buying designer clothes for a while or taking lunch to work, buying less phone cards for cell phone credit but you have to find a way. It was the late Jim Rohn's teaching on a child and a dollar that really opened my eyes to this habit in a meaningful way. Rohn, being a farm boy from Idaho, used farming to teach many lessons. Rohn asked, "If the farmer eats all the seed, will there be any for the next harvest? Will he allow his wife and children to eat the seed?" Of course not, no seed, no harvest.

The habit of saving is the first step to achieve financial well-being. Now, I am no financial expert but do the research and study those who are doing well financially. You might protest that you don't have enough so how can you save? Well there are persons who earn less than you and they save. Perhaps you are in debt and saving is difficult, believe me I can relate. However, if you are disciplined you can do it. If you fail to save you will never have enough to clear debts or make use of opportunities for the future and nothing will change. My mom is an expert saver. Had it not been for this habit she could not have helped us in times of need or have any thing for emergency. In terms of saving, try to have 3-6 month's salary set aside and assign a specific purpose to your saving. If you don't you will save and use it unwisely. Believe me, I have fallen into that ditch many times over. In order to see how you can save, track all your expenses and see where you can cut back and where you can trim expenses. Work out a system to also reduce your debt but make sure you save while you pay off your debt. I recommend listening to an audio, "The 4 Laws of Financial Prosperity" by Blaine Harris and Charles Coonradt, **to help you to get into financial shape.**

Lesson 59: Be Systematic in the Allocation of Your Funds

Jim Rohn teaches a 70:10:10:10 formula. Spend 70, give 10% to charity or church, save 10% and invest 10% to make a profit. Now maybe your financial position does not allow this but decide on a system and do it. What about 97:1:1:1. Over time it will accumulate and the earlier you begin the better. As a Christian I believe in giving God FIRST, then saving and then spending. Since I began this practice, giving God first 10% that is 10% to church, before paying my monthly bills, I have noticed amazing things have started to happen in opportunities and even persons paying for things for me and giving free travel. Now I have always been giving above and beyond the tithe but I did not necessarily do this first. For me this is a way to honour God and express my trust in his ability to provide for me. I believe if I honour him, he will honour me. Now is there anything magical about 10%? No but it is a well established system of financial prosperity or what I call an Ancient path to financial well-being.

You may not like this system but you need a system of saving before spending. The system I support is 80:10:10. I am now disciplining myself to live by this; 10% to God and 10% to save and 80% to spend. I have heard of those who save 50% and spend 50%. There are even those who give away 90% and spend 10% like Rick Warren. You could practice having jars or envelopes for specific purposes and set aside specific amounts or percentages from your earnings or income to each jar or envelope for example, a jar for vacation, a jar for living expenses, a jar for charity, a jar for saving and a jar for investment. The point is you need a system of allocation of funds for your financial well-being.

LESSON 60: SAVE TO SOW (INVEST)

As I began searching for the secrets of financial well-being, I ran into some audios by Tony Robbins which have been helpful. Robbins started out very poor and today is a multi-billionaire. When you have, like me, experienced days when you don't have anything in the fridge or can't find money to take the bus, you seek knowledge and a way out. When you have suffered the pangs of hunger and dread the end of each month, you search for answers. When you cannot give to the causes which are close to your heart, and see persons set back because of lack, you search for answers. Robbins has had those experiences but things have changed for him. One of the things he says is that you will not earn your way to financial independence. It is about compounding growth. In other words, it is the returns on your investment over time that will give you the financial rewards you are looking for and position you for financial independence. Robbins shares his secrets on wealth, success, and financial freedom in the book, *Money: Master the Game*.

Now if you have not saved anything you will not have anything to sow (invest). You need to sow and invest in things that will give you passive income or ongoing income. You not only reap what you sow but more than you sow. The trees teach us this all the time for example, when you plant one mango seed, you get a tree that bears many mangoes for several years and produces many more seeds. From these investments or the returns and wise use of your returns you will be in a position to give to the causes that you want to support. For me that is missions and investing in tertiary education of the poor. In order to give more, I need to have more or develop relationships with those who have more to be able to support these causes. It is clear that those who have more materially practise saving and sowing. Where to sow demands further research and thinking but I believe you get the idea. Once you have the desire and it's a burning desire, you will find a way.

IT'S TIME TO INTROSPECT

1. What ideas, beliefs or habits have contributed to you being financially unhealthy?
2. Will you discipline yourself and begin the habit of saving?
3. What steps will you take from now on to spend less than you earn?
4. If you are truly serious about being financially healthy, find a model to emulate. Seek advice and commit to a systematic plan for your financial well-being.

Where there is a will, you will definitely find a way. Stay tuned for tomorrow's tree talk as we enter the final of our tri-part series of talks on living successfully like trees.

RESPONSE TO TREE TALK

What actions will you take as a result of this tree talk? Or what decisions will you make?

PART III:
LIVE SUCCESSFULLY
LIKE TREES

*One that would have the fruit
must climb the tree.*
—Thomas Fuller

Recording My Tree Talks

TALK 21
RELEASING THE
TREASURE IN YOU

The tree of life was on each side of the river. It produces fruit twelve times a year, once each month. The leaves of the tree are for the healing of all the nations.
Revelation 22:2

Imagine, if you will, being on your death bed – And standing around your bed – are the ghosts of the ideas, the dreams, the abilities, the talents given to you by life. And that you for whatever reason, you never acted on those ideas, you never pursued that dream, you never used those talents, we never saw your leadership, you never used your voice, you never wrote that book. And there they are standing around your bed looking at you with large angry eyes saying we came to you, and only you could have given us life! Now we must die with you forever. The question is – if you die today what ideas, what dreams, what abilities, what talents, what gifts, would die with you?
—Les Brown

Each year more than 800,000 people commit suicide—around one person every 40 seconds. They choose not to live and many of their ideas, dreams, talents and gifts die with them, never ever seeing the light of day. In the 15 to 29-year age group, suicide is the second leading cause of death globally.[11] But one does not have to commit suicide to stop living; one simply has to give up or waste one's years with things that do not matter much earthly or eternally. This was almost my lot. I almost died without releasing the treasure in me, without making a valuable contribution to this world because I did not have a sense of purpose nor did I believe I was a very important or valuable member of society. I merely existed.

From the age of 10–17, I struggled with what is known as an existential crisis. I struggled especially with two questions: Who am I? Why am I here? At the age of 10, I was writing on walls: "I wish I was not born." By age 13, I tried to commit suicide. I took several pills from a bottle, waited to die but incredibly nothing happened. I think in hindsight they were vitamins and thus I did not get the intended overdose. Although I attended church and even got baptised, I did not understand my faith or purpose. By age 17 the crisis climaxed, I despised the dawn of each new day and begged God to let me die. I would ask him angrily each day, "why did you give me life?" I felt hopeless, useless, unwanted and unloved.

Nevertheless, it was in this state that something amazing happened that changed my life forever and set me on a new path to live meaningfully and to begin to release the treasures in me. Shortly before turning 18, I had a life changing encounter. A woman and two men spoke into my life. The lady spoke first saying: "God is about to remove your timidity and he is about to launch you into something new. He is going to use you. Get more of his

Word." The men told me that I would be used to help many people, that I would travel to several countries and become a minister. They even named some famous female ministers to give me an idea of how I would be used. They told me God would send me mentors and one of them said that my thinking was too small, that I should think big. He called me a champion. Many other things were said and I have not forgotten them. At that critical phase of my life I heeded their instructions and started developing the philosophy, habits and thoughts of successful people, all of which positioned me to begin to release the treasures in me. It was then that the desire for death left me and I became purpose driven. Their words charted me in a new direction and since that time I have become bolder, speaking to hundreds across the world and helping many people to live their dreams and make a difference in the world.

Now how does all of this relate to trees? There has been a move in recent years to intentionally go green to preserve the trees and make life much better on earth. We know that trees need to live because they make an invaluable contribution to our existence. Trees are treasures. Their value is without question. From the beginning, trees have been connected with our human existence. In fact, if we believe the creation story in Genesis, trees preceded our existence and are intricately connected with our lives. There was a tree of life in the Garden of Eden where the first humans resided and a tree of the knowledge of good and evil. While some believe that this is metaphorical, my point is: trees and humans are interconnected. Trees don't exist without reason and we have used trees in many beneficial ways. We have released the treasures of the trees and we should do the same with our lives. Here are three lessons on releasing the treasure in you just as we have with the trees.

LESSON 61: DON'T JUST LIVE; LIVE ON PURPOSE

How does one begin to release the treasures that are within? I believe it begins with **definiteness of purpose** and understanding what contributes to a meaningful life. It is what changed my life and what I believe will change yours. My questions to you are as follows:

- Are you living a meaningful life?
- Are you living a life worth living or merely existing: eating, drinking, paying bills, partying or something more?
- What treasures are within you that need to be released?

Myles Munroe, world renowned leadership expert, once said: "True leaders are born when you find something to die for... Most people die at age 25 and are buried at age 65...suicide is a permanent solution to a temporary problem. Everything in life will change so don't take yourself too seriously." Indeed I was taking myself too seriously. I was taking the comments of those at school and at home too seriously and I gave up. I am grateful it did not work because now life is exciting even during the hard days. Tough days don't last but tough people do. Again, another quote from Myles Munroe will suffice: "The wealthiest places in the world are not gold mines, oil fields, diamond mines or banks. The wealthiest place is the cemetery. There lies companies that were never started, masterpieces that were never painted... In the cemetery there is buried the greatest treasure of untapped potential. There is a treasure within you that must come out. Don't go to the grave with your treasure still within YOU."[12] I dare you to choose today to live on purpose.

LESSON 62: DON'T JUST LIVE; LIVE WITH PURPOSE

I heard John Maxwell, renowned author and leadership expert, say in a video on you-tube recently, that the two most important days of your life are: "the day when you were born and the day you discover why." What a profound statement! When you discover why you were born, it is then that you really start living with purpose. Purpose, according to Munroe, "is when you know and understand what you were born to accomplish. Vision is when you see it in your mind and begin to imagine it." Purpose and vision are interconnected. Again, Munroe's wisdom comes into play: "the greatest tragedy in life is not death but a life lived without purpose." When we live with purpose, we achieve more. We use our time better. We are able to focus better and give attention to things that really matter. If you don't live with purpose, you will be living out the purposes of other people and following their dreams or wasting your life.

I found the question asked in Jack Canfield's *Success Principles* very helpful in this seeking to live purposefully and earning an income. "What is a job I would love so much that I would do it for free but that I could actually get paid for? In *Success Principles*, Canfield explained that a lady named Julie asked this question and thought back over all the things she had done in her life and what had made her most happy. When she figured it out, she sought training and learnt how to monetize her gift. Julie became quite successful even working in the White House. This model is helpful. Living with purpose builds self-confidence. It determines where you live and with whom you interact. It affects our habits and choices. It was Benjamin Disraeli, former British Prime Minister who said: "the secret of success is the constancy of purpose." Purpose makes you unstoppable. Jim Rohn puts it like this, "when you know the why, the how gets easier." Purpose is the oxygen that keeps you breathing. It is the engine that keeps the car running. It is that which enables you to be resilient in the tough times. If you are going to release the treasure within you, you must be guided by purpose. I dare you today, to live with purpose.

LESSON 63: DON'T JUST LIVE; LIVE PASSIONATELY PURPOSEFUL

I recently heard a preacher say, "Purpose is the reason for the journey. Passion is the fire that lights the way." Passion and purpose are explosive when mixed together. Here are some quotes that highlight the importance of passionate living.

"The most powerful weapon on earth is the human soul on fire."
—Field Marshal Ferdinand Foch

"When you set yourself on fire, people love to come and see you burn."
—John Wesley, Evangelist (18TH century)

"One person with passion is better than forty people merely interested."   —E. M. Forster

"There is no greatness without a passion to be great, whether it's the aspiration of an athlete or an artist, a scientist, a parent, or a businessperson."   —Anthony Robbins

Jim Rohn captured it simply but profoundly: "Give everything you do all you've got. That's the secret of success." What dream do you need to become passionate about? What vision do you need to pursue passionately? What treasures are within you that need to come out?

IT'S DECISION TIME

Decisions shape your destiny.

1. *Decide today what to settle on? What is your chief definite purpose for living?*
2. *Decide today to do the things you are passionate and excited about.*
3. *Decide today to release the treasure within you.*
4. *Decide today to put your plans for the future on paper and begin to run with them.*

Where there is a will, you'll definitely find a way. Stay tuned for tomorrow's tree talk on making a valuable contribution.

RESPONSE TO TREE TALK

What actions will you take as a result of this tree talk? Or what decisions will you make?

TALK 22
MAKING A VALUABLE CONTRIBUTION

The great trees of Lebanon will be given to you: its pine, fir, and cypress trees together. You will use them to make my Temple beautiful, and I will give much honor to this place where I rest my feet.
Isaiah 60:13

VALUABLE CONTRIBUTION

I don't know about you but I just love homes with excellent landscaping! In fact, the property value for homes with excellent landscaping is usually higher than homes without. The property value of homes with well-maintained landscapes are up to 20% higher than others. Here are some eye-opening facts and statistics regarding the effect of healthy trees and shrubs on property value.

Homes with 'excellent' landscaping can expect a sale price 6-7% higher than equivalent houses with "good" landscaping. Improving "average" to "good" landscaping can result in a 4-5% increase. —Clemson University

99% of real estate appraisers concurred that landscaping enhances the sales appeal of real estate.

—*Trendnomics*, National Gardening Association

98% of realtors believe that mature trees have a "strong or moderate impact" on the saleability of homes listed for over $250,000 (83% believe the same for homes listed under $150,000).
—*American Forests*, Arbor National Mortgage

Landscaping can bring a recovery value of 100-200% at selling time. (Kitchen re: modelling brings 75-125%, bathroom re-modelling 20-120%.) —*Money Magazine*

I cannot say enough how valuable trees are. Trees not only have property value but they furnish us with life's essentials, food and oxygen. They provide shelter and medicine. Trees control climate by moderating the effects of the sun, rain and wind. Leaves absorb and filter the sun's radiant energy keeping things cool in summer. Trees also preserve the warmth by providing a screen from harsh wind. In addition to influencing wind speed and direction, they shield us from the downfall of rain, sleet and hail. Trees also lower the air temperature and reduce the heat intensity of the green greenhouse effect by maintaining low levels of carbon dioxide. Both above and below the ground, trees are essential to the eco-systems in which they reside. Far reaching roots hold soil in place and fight erosion. Trees absorb rain water which reduce runoff and sediment deposit after storms. This helps the ground water supply recharge, prevents the transport of chemical into streams and prevents flood.[13] But as valuable as trees are, humans are even much more valuable and we too have a great contribution to make in this world.

A PLEDGE OF CONTRIBUTION

I just love Jamaica's national pledge which is the perfect reminder that we have a valuable contribution to make in this world. Jamaica's national pledge says the following:

> Before God and all mankind, I pledge the love and loyalty of my heart, the wisdom and courage of my mind, the strength and vigour of my body in the service of my fellow citizens; I promise to stand up for Justice, Brotherhood and Peace, to work diligently and creatively, to think generously and honestly, so that Jamaica may, under God, increase in beauty, fellowship and prosperity, and play her part in advancing the welfare of the whole human race.

As students in school we had to recite this pledge. It is a vivid reminder that we have a valuable contribution to make in this world just like the trees. This is a pledge that can be universally applicable and help us to make a valuable contribution in life. Here now are three lessons on making a valuable contribution.

LESSON 64: YOU ARE A VERY IMPORTANT PERSON IN YOUR DESIGNER'S ECONOMY

You become what you think about. When you believe that you are an important person it will not be hard to see that you have a valuable contribution to make to society. It is a very important person who is expected to do things that will cause his country, family and community to increase in beauty, fellowship and prosperity. No designer or manufacturer makes junk. When your Divine Designer made you, he had an important purpose in mind, an important role for you to play. Furthermore according to the Genesis story of creation, he made humans in his own image and likeness and put them in charge of the earth. Great responsibility is not given to unimportant persons. Sometimes we fail to make the contribution we were designed to make because we feel unimportant and useless. You have something great to give to this world because you are a very important person in your Designer's economy.

LESSON 65: YOU SHOULD MAKE A VERY IMPORTANT PLEDGE OF CONTRIBUTION

If you will make this pledge and apply it to your life and nation, I am sure great things will happen. In order to make this pledge a reality, you will have to determine the part you will play. You need to analyze your gifts and ask the question: What can I do? Where do I want to make a contribution? How do I want to contribute? What am I here on earth to do? What mark do I want to make? What legacy do I want to leave? I love what Neil deGrasse said:

> "Who are we, if not measured by our impact on others? That's who we are! We're not who we say we are, we're not who we want to be—we are the sum of the influence and impact that we have, in our lives, on others."

The need to contribute is one of the highest goals in life. It increases the level of satisfaction we feel and it makes life meaningful. Work is a good thing and our worth may be a reflection of our work or what truly matters to us. You have work to do, an important contribution to make before you leave this world. Why not make a pledge to do it?

LESSON 66: YOUR VISION OF CONTRIBUTION IS POSSIBLE

If someone has done what you have conceived, it is possible. Even if no one has ever done what you have envisaged, the fact that it is in your heart means that it is possible. You may not know how at this point but it is possible. When Usain Bolt broke the world record, running 9.58 seconds, this was previously not thought as being possible. There was even a time when breaking the 10 second barrier in the 100m race was considered impossible but one day that record was broken and since then it has become normal for men to run sub ten seconds. When Alexander Graham Bell conceived of the phone many believed it was not possible. When the Wright brothers conceived of the aeroplane many had believed it was not possible. There were many who ridiculed these persons but they proved that a dream in the heart is possible. Whatever contribution you have envisaged is possible. All things are possible to the one who believes.

IT'S DECISION TIME

Decisions shape your destiny.

1. *Accept today the fact that you are an important person.*
2. *Decide today that you will make a valuable contribution in this world before you die.*
3. *Make a pledge today to run with your vision.*

Where there is a will, you will definitely find a way. Stay tuned for our next tree talk on confidence and self-worth.

RESPONSE TO TREE TALK

What actions will you take as a result of this tree talk? Or what decisions will you make?

TALK 23
CONFIDENCE AND SELF-WORTH

*How beautiful and how
delightful you are, My love,
with all your charms! Your
stature is like a palm tree.
[Song of Songs 7:6-7a]*

I will never forget a young man whose name is Andrew. He and I were in Teachers' College together. He was fairly tall, light-skinned and very handsome. I liked Andrew and I suspected he had eyes for me as well. Andrew was not only kind but a very sweet and wonderful person. We never did enter a romantic relationship and over the years whenever I see Andrew, he reminds me of something I said to him in college: "You're too good for me." Whenever I think about it, I feel a sting of pain and I wonder what my relational experiences would have been like if I had given Andrew a chance instead of all the others who broke my heart. My response revealed the depth of my low self-worth and confidence. How could I think Andrew was too good for me and on the flipside why did I not think I deserved someone as good as Andrew? Low self-esteem is a thief and robber. It often robs us of our potential and keeps us from releasing the treasures within us and making a significant contribution to our world. Now, what is the connection between trees and our self-worth and confidence?

Recently, I read phrases from Song of Solomon in the book *Healing for the Bruised Soul*, which makes clear the connection between trees and self-worth. "When I feel good about me I stand tall like a tree."[14] I have noticed that people who lack confidence generally have drooped shoulders, hang their heads down and don't like to look you in the eyes. Trees stand tall and magnificent. To stand tall also means to be brave and proud. It is to be confident of one's abilities. We should model trees in this regard. When we have low self-esteem or are filled with fear, we are not standing tall like trees.

Successful people are usually confident. Our confidence is based on our self-concept which is made up of all of our ideas, pictures, images, and especially our beliefs about ourselves. It affects how we manage all areas of our lives. How we think and feel about ourselves, says Brian Tracy, largely determines the quality of our life. Self-esteem is defined as "how much you like yourself." Your self-esteem is largely determined by the way you use your life and time in the development of your full potential. Your success is affected by how much you like yourself and as such we need to develop confidence and have a high sense of self-worth. Jim Rohn reminds us that: "The understanding of self-worth is the beginning of progress." Our self-worth has to do with the value we place on ourselves. When we see ourselves as valuable, then our confidence soars. Becoming confident is a skill that is learnable. Here now are three lessons in building self-worth and confidence.

LESSON 67: CONFIDENCE AND SELF-WORTH COME FROM YOUR CREATOR

I know of no manufacturer who spends time, effort and money into making junk. Whatever is created has a purpose and has value. In the same way, God makes no junk. Human beings are the crown of creation. We have more grandeur than anything in all of creation. We were made in God's image and likeness and therefore there is no place for low self-esteem or having a low value of ourselves. It matters not where we are from, our social class or financial status. For sure our value in the market place differs but we should not confuse that with our inherent value and worth. In Christian theology, Jesus died for us while we were yet sinners and rebellious, when we were his enemies. Who would die a cruel death for someone who is not valuable? Who would think precious thoughts about someone who is not valuable? Psalm 139 says we are fearfully and wonderfully made and God's thoughts towards us are precious and they outnumber the sand on the seashore.

I grew up in a poor family and was raised in the inner city community of Olympic Gardens, in Kingston, Jamaica, from the age of 10. I felt for a long time because of my social status and where I was raised that I was inferior and did not have much value. As a result, I settled for mistreatment when I should not have and did not dream big. Then I read that Jesus was from Nazareth, a place where no-one thought anything good came from. I also read he was placed in a manger as a baby. A manger is an animal's feeding trough. I also realized that He was still king while in the manger and he was still someone great and destined for greatness in spite of his earthly origin. Many of his Apostles came from places of low esteem and yet he chose them and used them to transform the world. Our self-worth is not diminished because others fail to recognize it. It is not dependent on possessions, achievements origin or social class but is based on the purposes and thoughts of the one who created us. You have been made just the way you are to fulfil a specific purpose. There is no need to downgrade yourself or wish you were someone else. When we realize that the Creator said, "very good" after creating us, our confidence rises. When our confidence rises, so does our ability to achieve our goals and reap success.

LESSON 68: CONFIDENCE AND SELF-WORTH RISE WITH CLARITY AND CERTAINTY

When you are clear and certain about your identity, purpose or what you desire, you will indeed feel and act with greater confidence. When you are certain of the expectations of your workplace or your family, it automatically leads to more confidence and greater productivity. When you are clear on your goals or your destination, once again, you move and act with confidence. Fear, the opposite of confidence is closely related to doubt and uncertainty. We tend to fear that which we do not know or are unsure of. In fact, success expert, Brian Tracy, posits that clarity is the starting point of all success. Clarity is the ability to decide what you want to be, do and have in life. Without clarity there is no sense of direction and when we lack a sense of direction, we will lack confidence. Your confidence and sense of self- worth will rise when you operate with clarity and confidence.

LESSON 69: CONFIDENCE RISES WITH COMPETENCE

Have you ever noticed the fear or insecurity on the faces of new employees at the bank or in a restaurant? I notice that the manner in which they speak and act betray immediately that they are new and unsure of themselves. In contrast, those who have been there a while act with greater certainty and speak more confidently. In fact, the higher the status of the employee, the more confidently they speak. According to Brian Tracy,

> ...your self-esteem and confidence increase when you are working efficiently, and your self-esteem goes down when you are not. The flip side of the coin of self-esteem is called "self-efficacy," defined as the degree to which you feel you are competent, capable, and productive, able to solve your problems, do your work, and achieve your goals. The more competent, capable, and productive you feel, the higher your self-esteem the more productive and capable you will be. Each one supports and reinforces the other.[15]

If you want to increase your confidence become a master in an area. Increase your knowledge, skills and practice. Not only will you become more confident but your worth and value in the market place will increase and you will reap greater rewards. Is it time to go back to school? Why not devote time to developing your knowledge and skills by reading more or listening to audio programmes? Why not do some volunteer work to get more experience?

IT'S DECISION TIME

Decisions shape our destiny.

1. *Make a decision today to become more confident. Do a study of self-confidence and take a confidence assessment test. Brian Tracy has such a test. Visit his website at http://www.briantracy.com/new/success/self-confidence/the-confidence-factor-a/ to learn more. This will help you to determine where you are and how much more you need to learn.*
2. *Examine your life today and determine in which area you need to become more competent and take action today to develop more competence in that area.*
3. *Decide today to act with clarity and certainty whatever the project, whatever the decision and in all areas of your life. Focus on getting clarity before you act and your rate of success will increase.*

Where there is a will, you will definitely find a way. Stay tuned for our next tree talk on setting life management goals and setting priorities.

RESPONSE TO TREE TALK

What actions will you take as a result of this tree talk? Or what decisions will you make?

TALK 24
LIFE MANAGEMENT AND SETTING PRIORITIES

They will not build and another inhabit, They will not plant and another eat; For as the lifetime of a tree, so will be the days of My people, and My chosen ones will wear out the work of their hands.
Isaiah 65:22

Ever since I became part of the Jamaican Green Smoothie movement, I have paid close attention to the fruits in season. Knowing which fruit is in season is absolutely essential to maintaining an affordable smoothie habit. When the fruit is in season, it is easier to get free fruits instead of always buying and the cost of the fruit is usually more affordable because of a glut on the market. Mangoes, which are my favourite fruit, are not always in season like the starfruit but sometimes for weeks after the fruit season is over I still have mangoes to make delicious smoothies because either I, my neighbour or my landlady found a way to preserve them. In the same way, we too must prepare for the seasons of our lives. Like trees we all have different seasons. Sometimes it is planting time; sometimes it is reaping time and sometimes waiting and watching time. We must learn to manage the seasons of our lives and more importantly we must learn to manage our days and our weeks. Time management, says Brian Tracy, is life management. Trees are excellent at time management. Due to their inbuilt plan and design trees know exactly what to do and when to do it to be productive. If trees can master the seasons and prepare for the seasons, certainly we too can master the seasons and manage our time in a manner that will lead to maximum productivity, happiness and success. Here are three lessons on life management or personal time management.

Lesson 70: Set Priorities Based on Your Life Purpose

"Things which matter most must never be at the mercy of things which matter least."
—*Johann Wolfgang von Goethe*

Von Goethe is right and I have found Brian Tracy's writings on time management quite useful in this regard. Here is what Tracy says in learning to prioritize. Tracy notes that a major reason for personal stress and unhappiness is the feeling that what you are doing has no meaning and purpose as it applies to you and your innermost values and convictions. He recommends that we start off by asking the question, "Why?" By asking why questions we can become more efficient with time management techniques because it won't do you any good if you just become more efficient at doing something that is meaningless to you.

Here are some priority questions that Tracy believes will help you.

What do you value most in life? What do you really care about and stand for? What will you not stand for? Why am I doing what I am doing? Why do you get up in the morning? Why do you do the job you do? What is your reason for working where you work? You will only feel really happy, valuable, and worthwhile to the degree to which your day-to-day activities are in harmony with your values. Almost all stress, tension, anxiety, and frustration, both in life and in work, comes from doing one thing while you believe and value something completely different.[16]

For more on time management I recommend Tracy's books: Time Management and Eat That Frog. Know what you want and why you are here. Know what you are trying to accomplish. Knowing these things will help you set your priorities and will certainly help you to manage your time and life better.

LESSON 71: PRACTICE THE PARETO PRINCIPLE

The Pareto principle is named after an Italian economist, Vilfredo Pareto. After years of research he discovered that 20 percent of individuals and families-those he called the "vital few" controlled 80% of the wealth and property in Europe. This 80/20 rule can be applied to our tasks and responsibilities and many areas of our lives. 20% of our activities is responsible for 80% of our success. This means only the 2 of your 10 top goals will give you the greatest success. Only two activities out of your day will be responsible for most of your success. Only 20% of the company really contributes to the company's success in really meaningful ways. Once you discover what those two things are on a daily basis, do them. Focus most of your attention on these areas. If it is relationships, do the same.

With whom are you spending time? Are you spending most of your time with the people who matter most or on the things which matter most? If you are young are you spending more time on social media networks, video games or playing games than you are with trying to get a good education or laying the foundation for a better future? To what are you giving the most attention? What you focus on the most is what you will bring about. Be wise in the use of your time. All of us have the same 24 hours, whether rich or poor, the difference is in how we choose to use them. Why not make a list of the 10 things that really matter; the results that really matter at home, work or school? Then see what two things in each of those two lists will help you to reap the best results. Spend most of your time on those two things. Let the Pareto Principle work for you today. Try it! What do you have to lose by trying?

LESSON 72: PRIOR PROPER PLANNING

Prior proper planning prevents poor performance. Here is a technique in prior proper planning that will help you to better manage your life and time. The story is told by Earl Nightingale on Nightingale Conant as follows:

> The president of a big steel company had granted an interview to an efficiency expert named Ivy Lee. Lee was telling his prospective client how he could help him do a better job of managing the company, when the president broke in

to say something to the effect that he wasn't at present managing as well as he knew how. He went on to tell Ivy Lee that what was needed wasn't more knowing but a lot more doing. He said, "We know what we should be doing. Now if you can show us a better way of getting it done, I'll listen to you and pay you anything within reason you ask."

Well, Lee then said that he could give him something in 20 minutes that would increase his efficiency by at least 50 percent. He then handed the executive a blank sheet of paper and said, "Write down on this paper the six most important things you have to do tomorrow." Well, the executive thought about it and did as requested. It took him about three or four minutes.

Then Lee said, "Now number those items in the order of their importance to you or to the company." Well, that took another three or four or five minutes, and then Lee said, "Now put the paper in your pocket. And the first thing tomorrow morning take it out and look at item number one. Don't look at the others, just number one, and start working on it. And if you can, stay with it until it's completed. Then take item number two the same way, then number three, and so on, till you have to quit for the day.

"Don't worry if you've only finished one or two; the others can wait. If you can't finish them all by this method, you could not have finished them with any other method. And without some system, you'd probably take 10 times as long to finish them and might not even have them in the order of their importance. Do this every working day," Lee went on. "After you've convinced yourself of the value of this system, have your people try it. Try it as long as you like. And then send me your check for whatever you think the idea is worth."

The entire interview hadn't taken more than a half-hour. In a few weeks the story has it that the company president sent Ivy Lee a check for $25,000 with a letter saying the lesson was the most profitable, from a money standpoint, he'd ever learned in his life. And it was later said that in five years this was the plan that was largely responsible for turning what was then a little-known steel company into one of the biggest independent steel producers in the world. One idea, the idea of taking things one at a time in their proper order. Of staying with one task until it's successfully completed before going on to the next.[17]

I personally practice this idea of single handling and planning in advance. I find that it really helps me to manage my life better. Fruit trees plan in advance for the fruit season. They know when to shed leaves, when to blossom and when to ripen. If we fail to plan, we simply plan to fail. Success is always intentional. No one makes a building without first creating a design, a blueprint. We should do the same with our lives. Prior proper planning includes setting time for rest, recreation and time with loved ones, not just time to work and make a living. Prior proper planning also includes time to serve others, to help humanity. Now, when doing this we should be flexible because things do not always turn out as planned. However, it is better to be prepared for an opportunity and not have one than to have an opportunity and not be prepared. We must be intentional. If we are casual about things we will end up a casualty.

IT'S DECISION TIME

1. *Decide today what your priorities are regarding your career, family, physical and spiritual health. Put these on paper.*
2. *Decide today to apply the Pareto principle and to find out more about time management.*
3. *Decide today to plan your days, weeks, months and even years in advance. Be flexible, adaptable and teachable, along the way.*

Where there is a will, you will definitely find a way. Stay tuned for our next tree talk on networking for success.

RESPONSE TO TREE TALK

What actions will you take as a result of this tree talk? Or what decisions will you make?

TALK 25
NETWORKING FOR
YOUR SUCCESS

He also took some of the seed of the land
and planted it in fertile soil He placed it
beside abundant waters; he set it like a
willow. Then it sprouted and became a low,
spreading vine with its branches turned
toward him, but its roots remained under
it. So it became a vine and yielded shoots
and sent out branches.
Ezekiel 17:5-6

I have been carefully observing my neighbour's
East Indian mango tree for some time now. In fact, I
have been counting and eagerly watching the development of the mangoes which are growing close to
our side of the fence. Some of the mangoes are now
ripe and I am ecstatic! I wait in anticipation for one
to drop. Those close to the fence I pick and enjoy to
my heart's content. I make green smoothies with
them or eat them as they are. However, this enjoy-
ment was not possible one year ago because my
neighbour, as you may recall from a previous talk,
had cut the branches. When the branches were cut,
no fruit was able to grow. This has taught me a
valuable lesson about producing fruit and the
importance of branches and parts of the tree.

A tree has different parts: the root, the trunk,
the branches, the leaves and the fruit. Each part

has its function and each part is dependent on the other parts of the tree to function well. Fruits do not grow on the trunk of a tree. Branches which are not attached to the trunk cannot bear fruit. In fact, if the branches are few, chances are the number of fruit produced will be limited. As I have seen from observing my neighbour's mango tree, the wider the network of branches the more fruit that is produced. In the same way, successful people realize the importance of having many branches and networking with others. Research has found that networking can lead to people performing better at work and increases the chance of landing a job. Networking helps our successful people be more innovative and more productive. Today we will highlight valuable lessons on networking to fuel our success.

LESSON 73: FORM A MASTERMIND ALLIANCE

To network is to interact with others, to exchange information and develop professional or social contacts. Napoleon Hill, in his book *Think and Grow Rich*, highlights the importance of having a mastermind alliance as a key principle of success. Hill confirmed what God revealed in Genesis 11 about the power of working together for a common purpose. The people set out to build a tower to reach heaven and to build a name for themselves in disobedience to God's instructions. When God saw how unified they were, having one language and one common purpose, he said nothing they think of will be impossible for them. Thus, he confused them by giving them different languages and the project was abandoned. The place was called Babel.

When we form an alliance of people of like mind and purpose we will accelerate our progress. The master mind group should not only have persons who have similar purpose and speak a common language but they should have skills that will complement one another. The members should have different areas of expertise that will complement and benefit the other members of the group so that together everyone can achieve success. As you consider this concept, ask yourself with whom should you form a mastermind alliance? Les Brown once said: "if you are the smartest one in your group, then you should consider getting another group." You not only become what you think about but you become like the people with whom you spend most of your time. With whom are you networking with or spending time?

LESSON 74: YOUR SUCCESS HINGES ON NETWORKING WITH OTHERS

In 2013, when I was leaving Namibia, Africa, I had to connect to a flight in Johannesburg and as I was leaving the airport, I noticed a sign on the wall that I have never forgotten. It read, "If you want to go fast, go alone. If you want to go far, go together." If you intend to have far reaching success, you need to network with others. You will never independently have all the resources you need to achieve everything you want to achieve. At some point in time you will need the help of others in one way, shape or form. As a budding social entrepreneur I am very mindful of this. I will never impact all the people I want to impact without networking with others. True success depends on "other" power. Here is what I mean by this.

At some point on the journey, you will need *Other People's Knowledge (OPK); Other People's Experience (OPE); Other People's Money (OPM); Other People's Success (OPS);* be cognizant of *Other People's Failures (OPF); Other People's Contacts (OPC)* and the list goes on and on and the greater your vision, the more people you will need in your network. The capacity of a tree to bear fruit hinges on the strength of its root system and the strength of its branches. In the same way the magnitude of your success hinges on the strength of your root system and the width, height and depth of your network. KFC and other business owners know this principle very well. It is the KFC chain, franchise or network in many countries that contributes to the company's massive earning power and success. How will you apply the principle of networking for your success?

LESSON 75: NETWORK FOR GREATER ACHIEVEMENT

When we network with others, our capacity for growth is exponential. Often times those with whom you network have resources that you don't have which you need to achieve your goal. For example, the Child Resiliency programme of which I am a part, uses the property of the YMCA to conduct its operations. This saved the developers of the programme the task of finding resources to establish facilities for the programme. Indeed, it is true: Together Everyone Achieves More (TEAM). Sometimes those you network with have resources, ideas, systems, platforms, models etc, that you do not have or cannot afford to establish or purchase, but need. In this case, there is no need to reinvent the wheel if someone already has what you need. Find a way to network, to share resources, to complement each other for greater achievement.

IT'S DECISION TIME

Decision shapes destiny!

1. *Make a decision today to network with others and to strengthen your network.*
2. *Make a list today of all the people you can form a mastermind alliance with and why you want to network with them. Form a mastermind alliance in the next few weeks.*
3. *Make a list today of resources you need that others have and find a way to network with those who have what you need or those who can help you achieve your goals.*

Where there is a will, you will definitely find a way. Stay tuned for our next tree talk on accessing and receiving resources.

RESPONSE TO TREE TALK

What actions will you take as a result of this tree talk? Or what decisions will you make?

TALK 26
ACCESSING AND RECEIVING RESOURCES

*The king made silver as common as
stones in Jerusalem, and he made
cedars as plentiful as sycamore trees
that are in the lowland.*
1 Kings 10:27

IT'S TIME TO TAKE ACTION

I've never seen a tree bringing me a fruit. If I want to make banana porridge I can't ask the banana tree to bring me bananas. If I want to eat a breadfruit I can't ask the breadfruit tree to bring it to me because I've never seen a tree with legs and arms. To get what I need from a tree I have to take initiative by either asking someone to go to the tree for it or climb the tree myself or wait till it drops a fruit for me to pick up and eat. Too many of us are waiting for handouts and Mr. Luck to throw resources and in particular money at us when there truly is no shortage of resource. "ALL I HAVE NEEDED, THY HAND HATH PROVIDED..." This is a line from one of the great hymns of the Christian faith, "Great is thy faithfulness. This line echoes my belief that truly there is no shortage of resources on earth to live the good life the Creator intended for us. What we are short on is access and the wisdom to access the resources we need.

In fact, II Peter 1: 3 indicates that His divine power has given us everything for life and godliness and goodness. While some of the greatest resources are free for example, the earth, the air we breathe, the trees, our bodies and the brain within the body, others are not but they are accessible. The question is how? Far too many of us fail to achieve our dreams or accomplish our God given design because we say we have no resources or money. There is no shortage of money. Many athletes, sports men and women, Hollywood actresses, entertainers and business men are earning millions of dollars. Many of them started with nothing but their gifts and abilities made room for them to access the resource from those who possessed it and so can we.

The formula for accessing resource can be found in Matthew 7: 7-8: "Ask, and God will give to you. Search, and you will find. Knock, and the door will open for you. Yes, everyone who asks will receive. Everyone who searches will find. And everyone who knocks will have the door opened."Access is reserved for the askers, seekers and knockers. This formula also gives us our three lessons for today.

LESSON 76: RECEIVING IS RESERVED FOR THE ASKERS; ASK AND IT SHALL BE GIVEN

My stomach echoed noises of dissatisfaction having not eaten anything all morning. I had just delivered the graduation address at an early childhood institution and now I needed to rendezvous with my mom by 1 p.m. so that together we could journey to Clarendon to deliver yet another motivational talk set for 4p.m. I needed to eat before the rendezvous because with our schedule we might not have another meal until 8p.m. Eating at the hospital, our rendezvous point, was out of the question. Eating in the bus park seemed out of the question and it made no sense visiting my friends in Hagley Park Plaza just to eat and then return to the same bus park. The pangs of hunger prolonged and so did my mind storm. Where am I going to eat? What am I going to eat?

While thinking about these questions, I took a taxi to Half Way Tree and made my way to a takeout restaurant in the Half Way Tree Transport Center and ordered some curried goat and rice and peas with steamed vegetables. Now with food in hand I reviewed my choices. The restaurants and pastry shops in and around this area do not permit eating unless you purchase the food from them. Where shall I eat? I cannot stand and eat. What shall I do? Suddenly a few wonderful phrases popped in my head as I saw an empty white chair in the little takeout centre, and noted that the employees in the centre worked mostly on their feet with obviously little room for seating. Receiving is reserved for the askers. *Ask and it shall be given. Everyone who asks receives.*

I then put on my brightest smile and asked if I could borrow the chair and sit at the back entrance of the serving depot to eat. Much to my delight, one of the employees responded affirmatively to my unusual request. She noted that this was not normative but extended the courtesy. I was relieved and delighted and left with an unforgettable lesson: *garner the courage to ask. What else could I have gained if I had the courage to ask more often? What opportunities have I missed out on for failure to ask? What new delights await me from the courage to ask?*

The courage to ask is vital to accessing resources when you don't have what you need. The courage to ask is a master key to opening doors to our success. Please note that while we do not always get what we ask for, if we do not ask, we run the risk of not receiving anything at all. Furthermore, when you ask, you need to ask intelligently, ask repeatedly, ask specifically, ask boldly and expect to receive. If you don't have the resource, find those who do and ask. Rise above the fear of rejection and ask. If you never ask chances are you will never receive. Give yourself a chance to receive. Ask for help, ask for opportunities, ask for advice, ask God for wisdom, knowledge and understanding, ask for strength, ask about how things are done. I want to challenge you today to ask. Muster the courage to ask and get answers to some of those nagging questions. Muster the courage to ask for the resources you need and get ready for some exciting responses and some surprising benefits! Receiving is reserved for the askers!

LESSON 77: FINDING IS RESERVED FOR THE SEEKERS; SEEK/SEARCH AND YOU SHALL FIND

Remember, you can't just sit and expect the mango to come to you and neither can you expect the resource you need to just come to you. Since there are resources available it makes sense to search and seek them out to find out how to access them. Seeking includes studying, researching on the internet, asking people who know more than you do, reading books, investigating and getting all the information you can to access the resource. Sometimes that information will lead you to create a product to access the resource or to develop a skill to access the resource. Study how people access resources, seek out the resources and as surely as you seek you will find answers to access what is required.

LESSON 78: OPEN DOORS ARE RESERVED FOR THE KNOCKERS; KNOCK AND THE DOOR SHALL BE OPENED UNTO YOU

Are people usually admitted to a school without applying? Do you usually get a job without applying? Knocking on doors means we seek opportunities. If you never try out for the football team chances are you will never make the team. It is the same with receiving and accessing resources. Opportunity comes to those who will knock. If you run out of supplies, go elsewhere. If your business is not doing well in one location, try another. In this regard persistence will be crucial. Knocking demands tenacity and sagacity because sometimes the doors will slam in your face but eventually a door will open and it could be the ticket to your dreams. Christian evangelists often use this verse when encouraging people to accept Jesus as their Saviour. Jesus said in Revelation 3:20: "Behold, I stand at the door and knock. If anyone hears My voice and opens the door, I will come in to him and dine with him, and he with Me." Open doors are reserved to the knockers. Will you knock on some doors today? You may just access and receive some well needed resources.

IT'S DECISION TIME

Decisions shape destiny.

1. *Will you ask, seek and knock today?*
2. *Do you know specifically what you need and how much you need?*
3. *Will you ask, seek and knock in faith expecting to receive?*

Where there is a will, you will definitely find a way. Stay tuned for our next tree talk on models of success

RESPONSE TO TREE TALK

What actions will you take as a result of this tree talk? Or what decisions will you make?

TALK 27
MODELS OF SUCCESS

*They will be like a tree planted by the
water that sends out its roots by the
stream. It does not fear when heat comes;
its leaves are always green. It has no
worries in a year of drought and never fails
to bear fruit... He is like a tree planted by
streams of water that yields its fruit in its
season, and its leaf does not wither. In all
that he does, he prospers.*
Jeremiah 17:8; Psalm 1:3

A model is a thing used as an example to follow or
imitate. From the aforementioned quotes, in the
books of Psalms and Jeremiah, the writers use trees
as models of prosperity, models of ongoing fruitfulness, models of peace and calm in the midst of
difficult situations and models of success. In my
quest to understand and achieve success, I have
found that in order to be successful it is important
to study models of success. Isn't it interesting that
trees are models of success, something whose
actions are worth emulating? And by the title of this
book, you know that this greatly excites me! Based
on these two quotes alone, being successful like
trees means being planted near a source of sustenance, being productive when we should be
productive and not wasting our lives. Our leaves
should not wither. We should always add value.

Being successful like trees means weathering adversity, eliminating fear and worry and not having excuses for our lack of productivity. Therefore as we look to the trees as models of success, here are three lessons to bear in mind: study models of success, adopt the attitudes of the models of success and adopt the philosophy of models of success.

LESSON 79: STUDY AND FOLLOW MODELS OF SUCCESS

Recently some friends and I were travelling to Ocho Rios in St. Ann by a route we had never previously taken. We decided to ask a taxi driver for direction and he simply said, "follow me" and with that we successfully arrived at our destination. When someone is new to a territory, having a travel guide who knows the territory is absolutely essential. When you start a new job, having someone who has been in the position to instruct and guide you along the way as you learn is absolutely essential. It is the same with the journey to success or great achievement. The people who have achieved great things are great guides along this journey. Many have left their knowledge and strategies in books and many are not afraid to share their success strategies with you if you care or dare to ask. This is one of the greatest secrets of success: study and follow successful people.

In this regard, something Brian Tracy once said, serves as a guide. "All skills are learnable." The skills that result in success are learnable and the greatest way to learn these skills is to study successful people and do what they do. Of equal importance in this business of success is to note what failures do and not repeat their errors in judgment. A good way emulate the successful is to be mentored directly by successful persons and if we cannot be mentored directly, we can always read their books and make use of whatever we can find about them on the internet. In this regard I have several you-tube success mentors, whom I have never ever personally met. Some are deceased but their ideas and lives were captured by others and today I am benefitting from the ideas of men like Earl Nightingale and Jim Rohn.

LESSON 80: ADOPT THE PHILOSOPHY OF SUCCESSFUL PEOPLE

"As a man thinketh in his heart, so is he."
Proverbs 23:7

Our philosophy, that is, our thought system plays a crucial role in our achievements. People who are successful think in ways unsuccessful people do not. We therefore should make it our goal to find out how successful people think and then adopt these patterns of thinking. For example, successful people are possibility thinkers, they think big, they take personal responsibility for their actions and they have a philosophy of perseverance. Here now are some of the philosophies of success that I have adopted and I encourage you to do your own study and find successful philosophies that you can adopt:

"For things to change, you have to change"
—Jim Rohn

"It does not profit to gain the whole world and lose your soul."
—Jesus of Nazareth

"If you know the prize, you will pay the price."
—Jim Rohn

"You have greatness within you... it's possible."
—Les Brown

"The price of discipline weighs ounces. The price of regret weighs tonnes."   —Jim Rohn

"There is a seed of equivalent benefit in every circumstance."   —Napoleon Hill

"The greatest tragedy in life is not death but a life lived without purpose."   —Myles Munroe

"It is not what you get that makes you successful. It is what you become. Success is what you attract by what you become."   —Jim Rohn

"Fail early, fail often, but always fail forward."
—John C. Maxwell

"Your attitude, more than your aptitude, will determine your altitude."   —John C. Maxwell

LESSON 81: ADOPT THE HABITS OF SUCCESSFUL PEOPLE

The truth is that we really are the sum of our habits. Habits are behaviours that we acquire through repeated actions which may either break or make us. If we change our habits, our lives will change. It is therefore wise to study the habits of successful people and adopt these habits. I therefore challenge you to discover the habits of successful people and seek to adopt them. Here now are two of the habits that I have discovered that are common to successful people:

Successful people set goals in writing for their future and make plans to achieve them. In 1979, interviewers asked new graduates from the Harvard's MBA Program and found that

1. 84% had no specific goals at all,
2. 13% had goals but they were not committed to paper, and
3. *3% had clear, written goals and plans to accomplish them.*

In 1989, the interviewers again interviewed the graduates of that class. You can guess the results:

- The 13% of the class who had goals were earning, on average, *twice as much as the 84 percent who had no goals at all.*
- Even more staggering, the three percent who had clear, written goals were earning, on average, *ten times as much as the other 97 percent put together.*[18]

THEY DON'T WATCH TV; THEY READ

According to Thomas Corley, author of *Rich Habits: The Daily Success Habits Of Wealthy Individuals*, 67 percent of rich people only watch TV for one hour or less per day. Corley also found only 6 percent of the wealthy watch reality shows, while 78 percent of the poor do.

Additionally, 86 percent of the wealthy love to read with an impressive 88 percent claiming that they read for self-improvement for 30 minutes or more per day.[19] Now, that you know that habits make a difference, I want to challenge you to do your own study and make a decision to adopt the habits of successful people.

IT'S DECISION TIME

Decisions shape your destiny.

1. *Make a decision today to strive for success.*
2. *Make a decision today to study and emulate models of success.*
3. *Make a decision today to adopt the philosophy, habits and attitudes of successful people.*

Where there is a will, you will definitely find a way. Stay tuned for tomorrow's tree talk on cultivating character and integrity.

RESPONSE TO TREE TALK

What actions will you take as a result of this tree talk? Or what decisions will you make?

TALK 28
CULTIVATING CHARACTER AND INTEGRITY

So every good tree bears good fruit, but the bad tree bears bad fruit. A good tree cannot produce bad fruit, nor can a bad tree produce good fruit. Every tree that does not bear good fruit is cut down and thrown into the fire.
Matthew 7: 17-19

Can you imagine going to the mango tree expecting to find mangoes and end up seeing avocados? Now that would be crazy! Mango trees do not produce avocados. A good tree cannot produce bad fruit, nor can a bad tree produce good fruit. This characteristic of trees is the epitome of character and integrity. Now what kind of tree are you? Are you a good tree or a bad tree? Do you have character and integrity? There is no true lasting success without character and integrity. Now we are all a work in progress and all of us need to improve in these two areas because no human is perfect but we can strive to develop to the point where others recognize us as persons of character and integrity. As motivational speaker and author, Dr. Eric Thomas says, "Your gift may take you where your character cannot keep you." Don't let your gift take you where your character cannot keep you. Let your character match your gift. Abraham Lincoln said, "Reputation is the shadow. Character is the tree." Our character is much more than just what we try to display for others to see, it is who we are even when no one is watching. Good character is doing the right thing because it is right to do what is right.[20] Now let's dive into three lessons we can learn about cultivating character and integrity as we strive for success.

LESSON 82: CHOOSE YOUR NON-NEGOTIABLE VALUES TO GOVERN YOUR LIFE AND BUSINESS

I'm sure you have seen many organizations with a list of core values for example, honesty, integrity, creativity, accountability, diversity, respect etc. Core values are the fundamental beliefs of a person or organization. The core values are the guiding principles that dictate behaviour and action. It is these core values that will determine our character and whether or not we have integrity. Integrity is often listed as a core value if not the most important of all core values. Integrity means following your moral or ethical convictions and doing the right thing in all circumstances, even if no one is watching you. It is being honest and having strong moral principles. My core beliefs come from Christianity and I seek to emulate the beliefs and value system of Jesus and his apostles in all I do. It is an ongoing but necessary process of becoming. We cannot consistently act in a manner inconsistent with our beliefs. When we act in a manner that goes against our expressed value system, we get labelled as hypocrites and become untrustworthy.

No one wants to be in business or relationship with someone who is untrustworthy, unreliable and hypocritical. I remember when I was serving with Operation Mobilization and collecting funds for missionaries, I told the administrator of a church that I would send some information to her soon and her words left an indelible mark on my mind, "I trust you explicitly." To this today, I am amazed. Recently someone said to a friend of mine, "If you want something done, Cameka is the person to get it done." Now, I have a reputation to live up to and that is the kind I want to build. Results matter to me and honesty is one of my core values. What are your core values? It is those values that will attract people to you and help you to become truly successful. Success is not what you get but what you become.

LESSON 83: BUILD A BRAND OR REPUTATION OF INTEGRITY AND CHARACTER

Can you imagine going to a mango tree that looks like a Julie mango tree, which produces fruit looking and tasting like an East Indian mango! That would sure be strange. What about going to a Kentucky Fried Chicken restaurant and the chicken tastes like Popeye's or Island Grill's? I'm sure KFC would get many complaints and eventually lose customers. KFC has produced a recipe that has been replicated in every country with pretty much the same taste and results and when we go to KFC we know what we are getting. When we buy a Julie mango, we pretty much already know what we are getting and so it should be with us. That is what it means to have a brand or reputation of integrity. People should know what we are like and what to expect when they do business with us. Our word should be our bond. It's hard to stay in relationship with someone who keeps changing or is very unpredictable. It is frustrating doing business with persons who are not dependable and not knowing if they will deliver a quality product creates anxiety. What's your brand? What's your reputation? Are you paying attention to it? We need to set standards and keep them. This is what will attract people to us and fuel our success.

LESSON 84: INTEGRITY AND CHARACTER WILL BRING YOU GREAT REWARDS

Jim Rohn said it right, "success is what you attract by the person you become." Your gifts will make room for you but character and integrity will get the room furnished, well maintained and always available. People of integrity and character are like treasures. They are sought after. They are the kind of people you want to be in business and relationship with. They are the ones whose advice is readily obeyed, the ones who command respect and are rewarded greatly. They are the ones people will sacrifice for and follow unquestioningly. Think of people like Mother Theresa, Nelson Mandela, Martin Luther King and Jesus Christ of Nazareth. When Jesus said, "follow me" the disciples moved immediately, without any hesitation and that is what integrity does. Don't compromise your values. Live with integrity. Your gifts will make room for you and take you before kings. Your character and integrity will keep you in that circle and enlarge your borders and rewards.

IT'S DECISION TIME

Decisions shape destiny.

1. *Make a decision today to become a person of integrity and sound character.*
2. *Decide today what your core values are and build a brand around them.*
3. *Decide today that you will not compromise your value system.*

Where there is a will, you will definitely find a way. Stay tuned for our next tree talk on meaningful and successful living.

RESPONSE TO TREE TALK

What actions will you take as a result of this tree talk? Or what decisions will you make?

TALK 29
MEANINGFUL AND
SUCCESSFUL LIVING

And seeing a fig tree by the wayside, he
went to it and found nothing on it but
only leaves. And he said to it, "May no
fruit ever come from you again!" And
the fig tree withered at once.
Matthew 21:19

The story of the cursed fig tree has always fascinated and challenged me. One day Jesus and his disciples were passing a fig tree in the fig bearing season. Jesus was hungry and so he drew near the fig tree to satisfy his hunger only to be left bitterly disappointed. The fig tree did not have figs. Jesus subsequently cursed the fig tree and the next day to the disciples' amazement it dried up completely. The fig tree was expected to bear fruit, to be productive, to contribute meaningfully by providing food in due season. By its failure to provide food and bear fruit, it was wasting its life and therefore need not exist anymore.

What a challenge! This is why my chief definite aim in life is tied to empowering people to live the meaningful, productive and successful lives they were designed to live. Don't waste your life! Don't become a cursed fig tree! A barren tree is not useful and a fruitless life is a life wasted. The fig tree had a purpose and it failed to fulfil it. It had an assignment and it failed to fulfil it. Its existence was therefore meaningless. My questions to you therefore are as follows: are you living a meaningful and productive life? Are you living a successful life? What does it mean to live a successful and meaningful life? If trees are expected to live meaningfully and successfully how much more should we?

INGREDIENTS OF A MEANINGFUL AND SUCCESSFUL LIFE

To be meaningful is to have meaning, to be purposeful, significant, relevant, worthwhile and important. When we live with meaning and purpose, we look forward to getting up each day even in the face of challenges. I believe that a meaningful and successful life constitutes at least five things:

1. Deep connection with your Creator/Divine Designer
2. Contribution and service in the world
3. Healthy relationships with other humans
4. Understanding, loving and accepting yourself
5. Clarity of purpose or having a vision [design, blueprint] for your future

A meaningful and successful life is not necessarily being rich or famous. If this were so, we would not have so many famous and wealthy persons on drugs, alcohol or ending their lives so tragically such as Ernest Hemmingway, Whitney Houston, Robin Williams, Marilyn Munroe, Vincent Van Gogh and many others. I am not saying that there are not persons who are wealthy and happy but too many people equate success primarily with money. Although the preface of this book started with my financial woes, please be clear that I am not saying that success for me is merely gaining control over my finances, although that is one of my goals. What I am saying, is that riches and fame should not be the greatest measure of success and having them does not equate to living a meaningful life. The life of Mahatma Ghandi, Jesus of Nazareth and Mother Teresa are great reminders in this regard. Who is your model of success? What does living successfully and meaningfully look like to you?

My ultimate model of success and what it means to live a meaningful and successful life is the life of Jesus of Nazareth.

He grew up like a small plant before the Lord, like a root growing in a dry land. He had no special beauty or form to make us notice him; there was nothing in his appearance to make us desire him. He was hated and rejected by people. He had much pain and suffering... He will complete the things the Lord wants him to do. After his soul suffers many things, he will see life and be satisfied. Isaiah 53: 2, 3, 11.

He came from a place that people believed nothing good would come from. He overcame tremendous obstacles. Although he had no wealth of his own he had resources to complete his mission. He was sure of his life assignment, lived with purpose and completed his assignment while leaving others to carry on his mission. Using his model, here now are three lessons in living a meaningful, productive and successful life.

LESSON 85: MEANING IS WRAPPED UP IN MISSION

According to philosopher Dallas Willard, "meaning is not a luxury for us. It is a kind of spiritual oxygen we might say that enables our souls to live." Psychiatrist Viktor Frankly says it is "the primary motivational force in man." It is not enough to exist. We have need for something more. Human beings need to answer the question of "What am I here for?" When this question is not answered, we often feel our lives are being wasted. Without an answer to this question there is no looking forward to our mornings.

From conception, Jesus' mother knew his mission. From an early age Jesus knew his mission and when the end was near he knew he had completed his mission. The Apostle Paul had a similar experience in the final moments of his life, "I have fought the good fight. I have finished the course." What is that mission which will give meaning to your life? What do you feel you are here for? What is that assignment that you think could make your life meaningful? What do you do that brings a great deal of satisfaction or happiness? What do you want to be remembered for?

LESSON 86: COMPLETE YOUR LIFE MISSION

The fig tree learnt the hard way that it is simply not good enough to just be a fig tree. It needed to produce figs. The fig tree did not complete its assignment. It's not just the start that matters, finishing matters. The fig tree had a great start. It grew well. It became strong and had matured but it did not bear fruit. Once you know your life mission, organize all you do around it and get to work. Everything you do should be related to it and do everything you can to complete your mission. When you know your life mission it becomes the why behind everything you do. Gather the resources, skills and training to complete it. In fact simply knowing your life mission and acting in accordance with it often attracts the people and resources you need to fulfil it.

LESSON 87: FINISH WELL

I believe all of us like praise for a job well done. The fig tree did not get any praise because it did not finish well. Six of the most beautiful and challenging words in all of Scripture which the Divine Designer will say to some of his creatures are: "Well done, good and faithful servants." Those are words I desire to hear. Those are challenging words because it is not just about finishing but how you finish. It is not just about doing but doing well and being faithful to the end. Finishing matters! Along the way there will be obstacles but do not quit, finish your mission and don't just finish it, finish it well. Wouldn't it be great to be remembered as a faithful finisher?

IT'S DECISION TIME

Decisions shape your destiny.

1. *Make a decision today to go on a journey to discover your life assignment.*
2. *Make a decision today that once you discover your life assignment that you will complete it.*
3. *Make a decision today to be faithful and finish well.*

Where there is a will, you will definitely find a way. Stay tuned for our next tree talk on maximizing your potential.

RESPONSE TO TREE TALK

What actions will you take as a result of this tree talk? Or what decisions will you make?

TALK 30
MAXIMIZE YOUR
POTENTIAL

*But the godly will flourish like palm
trees and grow strong like the cedars
of Lebanon.
Psalm 92:12*

TALL TREES IN THE BACKYARD

How tall does a tree grow? A tree grows as tall as it
can grow. I've always admired the height of trees.
As I compared the height of the trees in my yard
and those of my neighbours, I saw that the neighbor's breadfruit tree is taller than my mango tree.
The neighbor's East Indian is taller than my Julie
mango tree. The pear tree is not as tall as the Julie
mango tree but it is way taller than the lime tree.
The banana tree is shorter than the ackee tree. The
Moringa tree is as tall as the palm tree. What is significant is that despite the sizes, all the trees are
fully developed. They have all reached their maximum height and are producing, and so it should be
with us as human beings. We should all strive for
maximum growth and production, to maximize our
full potential. While we may not all grow as tall as
the East Indian tree or the breadfruit tree, we
should aim to reach our full height.

To grow is to undergo natural development by
increasing in size or changing physically. It is to

get taller, larger, to fill out, to come into existence and develop, to reach maturity, to increase in amount or degree, to strive or to spring up. Personal development or personal growth is the process by which we increase in amount or degree our life skills so that we can maximize and deliver on our potential. It is a process of becoming all we can be for maximum productivity. Trees grow out of something, that is they develop or come into existence from something and so do we. Trees grow on something and gradually become more pleasurable and acceptable to all and so should we. Today we'll look at lessons in tree growth to maximize our potential.

LESSON 88: TREES GROW OUT OF CHALLENGING SITUATIONS AND SO DO WE

A seed once planted dies before it grows into a tree and produces fruit. Once planted it has to push from beneath the soil to go above ground. As a young tree develops, it has to reach for sunlight and it has to sink its roots deep so that it can have sufficient nutrients in the soil to survive and find a way to store water in times of little rain because it does not rain every day. It has to adjust to the climate and harsh weather conditions. It has to grow in strength to face up to the winds that blow so that it does not topple over. It grows out of challenges.

I have been fascinated by the fact that trees grow out of dirt but we don't call it dirt. We call it soil because it has nutrients that nourish the trees. It is our adversities or problems and our dirt that often force us to grow and become more. It is when we are challenged that we often rise to the occasion and become more much like a muscle in need of pressure to build. Those who are successful all face challenges which push them past their comfort zone. The successful ones had to learn vital skills to navigate through life in order to survive. It therefore means as painful as our trials and problems are, we should not despise them because they are the seeds and soil from which we grow out of and these are what push us towards maximum growth.

Now I understand what Jim Rohn meant when he said don't wish for less problems, wish for more wisdom and skills. Now I understand why James, the Apostle, teaches count it all joy when you fall into trials. Now I understand when Jim Rohn said go where the challenges are great because that is the only way to maximize our potential. Now I understand what Jesus meant when he said, unless a grain of wheat dies it cannot bring forth much fruit. Are you determined to grow out of the challenges you currently face? Will you see them as fuel to help you to maximize your potential?

LESSON 89: WATCH WHERE YOU GROW, WHAT YOU GROW ON AND WHAT YOU BECOME

Once again, the words of Rohn are worth noting here. "You must constantly ask yourself these questions: Who am I around? What are they doing to me? What have they got me reading? What have they got me saying? Where do they have me going? What do they have me thinking? And most important, what do they have me becoming? Then ask yourself the big question: Is that okay? Your life does not get better by chance, it gets better by change.[21] Here is another story that has fascinated me over the years which illustrates the point Rohn makes beautifully. It is about the farmer and the seed. A farmer went out to plant his seed. While he was planting, some seed fell by the road, and the birds came and ate it up. Some seed fell on rocky ground where there wasn't much dirt. Those seeds grew very fast, because the ground was not deep. But when the sun rose, the plants dried up because they did not have deep roots. Some of the seed fell among thorny weeds which grew and choked the good plants. Some other seed fell on good ground and began to grow. It got taller and produced a good crop. Some plants made 30 times more, some made 60 times more, and some made a hundred times more (Luke 8:4-15).

One of the lessons from this story is that where you grow and the soil you grow on will affect what you grow into or become. We are affected by nature and nurture. We all have gifts and potential to do great things like a seed but we don't all become what we were designed to become. If you walk with fools you will be a fool. If you keep company with the wise you will be wise. If you have successful friends chances are you will be successful. It is said you are an average of the 5 persons you associate with most often.

It is also important what you feed yourself with. Malnourished or undernourished people don't grow well. If you feed yourself positive things, you will become positive. If you feed yourself thoughts of limitations and have self-limiting beliefs, you will be limited and not achieve much. Remember, as Les Brown says, you should always have smarter people around you. Stay far away from toxic people. They will ruin your life and undermine your potential. Stay away from the doubters. Even Jesus could not do many miracles in places where there were people with little faith. If you want to maximize your potential, watch carefully where you grow, what you are growing on and what you are growing into or becoming.

LESSON 90: GROW UP IN ALL AREAS OF YOUR LIFE

Trees aim upward, towards the heavens or sky, as they strive for maximum growth. You should do likewise. Les Brown says: "shoot for the moon... if you miss, you will still land among the stars." Brown further states: "some people fail in life not because they aimed too high and missed but they aimed too low and hit." Successful people are big thinkers who aim high like trees. If you think small you will only achieve small things. If you think big, you achieve big things because you become what you think about.

Maximizing personal potential requires holistic growth and development. That is why personal development or personal growth includes the physical, spiritual, mental, emotional and social aspects of our lives. We need to maximize our potential in all these areas so that we can live a balanced life and attain true success. True success has earthly and eternal dimensions. The story told by the Master storyteller illustrates this point well.

The master storyteller once told a story about a rich man who had some land with a good crop. He thought to himself, what will I do? I have no place to keep all my crops. Then he said:"this is what I will do: I will tear down my barns and build bigger ones, and there I will store all my grain and other goods. Then I can say to myself, "I have enough good things stored for many years. Rest, eat, drink, and enjoy life!" But God said to the foolish man, "tonight your life will be taken from you, who will get those things you have prepared for yourself? This is how it will be for those who store up things for themselves and are not rich towards God (Luke 12:16-21). In aiming high like the trees, or seeking to maximize our potential, we should look heavenward while living on earth just like the trees. In so doing, we should be able to truly maximize our potential and become all we were meant to be.

IT'S DECISION TIME

1. *Make a decision today to live holistically.*
2. *Identify the areas of your life you are neglecting and make a plan to achieve balance.*
3. *Be cognizant of your surroundings. Do a check list to see if those with whom you associate are hindering or helping you to grow and take corrective measures.*
4. *View your challenges as of today with kind eyes. It is your challenges which will help you to grow. There is joy on the other side of pain.*

Where there is a will, you will definitely find a way. Stay tuned for our final tree talk on hope for the future.

RESPONSE TO TREE TALK

What actions will you take as a result of this tree talk? Or what decisions will you make?

TALK 31
HOPE FOR THE FUTURE

Hope deferred makes the heart sick,
but desire fulfilled is a tree of life.
Proverbs 13:12

There was once a great king, named David, whose life was filled with much adversity. His father did not think much of him and when the time came to select one of his sons as King, he never even bothered to present David. David nevertheless was chosen to be king as a teenager but he did not become king until age 30. He faced opposition from the then King on the throne who sought to kill him because of jealousy. As a soldier David fought many battles and won. David used the olive tree as his symbol of hope and future triumph over his foes when he said, "... but I am like an olive tree growing in God's Temple. I trust God's love forever and ever" (Psalm 52:8).

The olive tree today is still a symbol of hope and immortality. In the Genesis story of the flood in the Old Testament, a dove returns with a green olive branch to announce the end of the flood and to bring hope to those on-board the ark. As stated before in our second motivational talk, the roots of the olive tree are very deep so much so that it can survive all manner of damage. Burned, it sprouts again. Cut down, there is always hope that the tree will send up a new shoot, even after appearing to have been dead for years. It lives for centuries and thus is also a symbol of immortality. Attaching hope to the olive tree is quite fitting because hope is one of the three qualities which are eternal: hope, faith and love. Having hope is vital to achieve success. Here now are three lessons on hope and success.

LESSON 91: HOPE KEEPS THE DREAM OF SUCCESS ALIVE AND MAKES THE PRESENT BEARABLE

Hope may be defined as having a confident expectation of the future. It is that which sees the invisible and makes the invisible visible. No one hopes for that which he already possesses. If you do not have hope, the goal will not be achieved. According to John Maxwell, "Where there is no hope in the future, there is no power in the present... Man can live 3 days without water; 40 days without food but cannot live 4 minutes without hope." I fully concur. Without having something promising to look forward to, you cannot survive struggles that you will face on the journey to success. When there is a positive expectation of the future, like the phoenix you can rise from the ash of failure. Hope energizes us and lifts us up out of the pit of despair. When we have a compelling picture of the future, it makes the pain of the present bearable because as the late Jim Rohn said, "If you know the prize, you will pay the price. If the promise of the future is clear, then you will pay the price."

LESSON 92: HOPE COMES FROM KNOWING YOU HAVE DIVINE AID

The concept of a Divine, all powerful being, on my side and ready to help me in times of need gives me great hope. "God is our refuge and strength, a very present help in times of trouble," (Psalm 46: 1). So we can say with confidence, "The LORD is my helper, so I will have no fear..." (Hebrews 13: 6). If my vision is from Him, then nothing can thwart his purposes. My dream may be delayed but not denied because no good thing will He withhold from those who walk uprightly (Psalm 84:11). What our Divine Designer wills, He builds. In fact our Divine Designer is the God of all hope and comfort (2 Corinthians 1:3). This has been my greatest inspiration in pursuing my life goals. I have Divine aid and thus success is possible.

LESSON 93: NEVER, EVER, EVER, EVER LOSE HOPE!

If you lose hope, you will never succeed, so never, ever, ever, lose hope! Keep the vision before your eyes. Do not grow weary of well doing for in due time you will reap a great harvest if you do not give up. Who has accomplished your dream? Find out and study how they handled obstacles and learn from them. If what you are striving for has already been done, then you can do it! Stay the course. Cry if you must but give birth. When you see the baby, the memory of the pain will disappear. There is joy on the other side of pain. Take heart from the words of Winston Churchill, former British Prime Minister in World War II, as he addressed the House of Commons, May 13, 1940, "You ask, what is our aim? I can answer in one word: Victory. Victory at all costs —Victory in spite of all terror—Victory, however long and hard the road may be, for without victory there is no survival."[22] Now I say without hope there is no success, so never, ever, ever, lose hope! Your dream is possible!

IT'S DECISION TIME

Decisions shape your destiny.

1. *Decide today that you will not give up on your dream.*
2. *Decide today like King David to seek Divine aid to achieve your goals.*
3. *Decide today to find models of hope to fuel your success.*

Where there is a will, you will definitely find a way. We've come to the end of our tree talks but we still have a treat for you. Turn the pages for *7 Life Changing Habits to Fuel Your Success* and a final word.

RESPONSE TO TREE TALK

What actions will you take as a result of this tree talk? Or what decisions will you make?

BONUS SECTION:
HABITS TO FUEL YOUR SUCCESS

7 Life Changing Success Habits

What's Your Destination?

Five years from now you will arrive at a destination. The question is: where? Where you arrive depends on the choices you make and steps you take in a particular direction. Your direction determines your destination. Our habits are steps which lead to certain destinations and the secret of success is in our daily routine and habits. Strong trees do not grow overnight and neither will you. Trees do not bear fruit overnight. Success is cumulative. Days lead to weeks, weeks lead to months and months lead to years and years lead to a lifetime. Our weekly routine needs to reflect the philosophy, attitude and habits of highly successful people. Success and leadership expert John Maxwell is a proponent of the Rule of 5 which is a key to success.

The Rule of 5 is simply a series of activities that you do EVERY DAY that are fundamental to your success. Maxwell uses the example of chopping a tree with an axe five times daily. He says eventually the tree will fall if one keeps chopping. It is simply a matter of time if one does this consistently. In the same way successful people have successful habits that lead to their success. Maxwell's personal Rule of 5 are as follows: *every day he reads, every day he files, every day he thinks, every day he asks questions and every day he writes.* I want to encourage you to develop your rule of five habits that will lead to your success. Here are seven life-changing habits that have helped me and many successful persons to achieve our highest life goals and have enabled us to live a more enriching and rewarding life.

LESSON 94: DAILY TIME WITH MY DIVINE DESIGNER

Abraham Lincoln's philosophy of success has guided me well in developing this habit and reminds me of the source of true success. According to Lincoln, "Without the assistance of that divine being, I cannot succeed. With that assistance I cannot fail. Trusting in Him, who can go with me, remain with you and be everywhere for good, let us confidently hope that all will yet be well." One of my habits is to spend time with God in prayer daily, acknowledging my dependence on him for strength, guidance and support. When I spend time in solitude with God, I get vision, ideas and plans. I realize that the plans and power emanate from my time with Him. I take a notepad with me in these times of solitude to write down the thoughts and ideas which come to mind. When I act on these ideas I usually reap success.

Sometimes my time of solitude with God is short and sometimes it is extended through fasting and prayer. I find extended periods of prayer and reflection extremely rewarding. My blog ideas usually emerge from these times and projects that I have executed such as my Taste of Africa fundraising event in 2013 which yielded almost US$6000.00 and my *Design to Win* mentoring programme as well as my first book. The messages I deliver at different speaking events usually emerge from these times of solitude with my Divine Designer and most importantly, I find peace in the midst of storms when I take my concerns to Him, in these times of solitude and prayer. Truly, I know I can do nothing without Him and through Christ who strengthens me I can do all the things that I need to do.

LESSON 95: LIFE DESIGN TIME

Without vision people perish. I believe in writing the vision and making it plain on paper. This is similar to a designer creating a sketch or blueprint for a product to be created. Architects have blueprints and fashion designers have their sketches and so should we for our lives. The design for my life is envisioning what I want to become, do, be, have, see and the impact I want to create or the legacy and mark I want to leave on this earth after I die. This is the time to set your most important life goals and to work on them year by year, month by month and day by day. Some people create vision boards and I do too. I rewrite my life major goals or my yearly goals on a daily basis. I find in doing this, I accomplish more and remain focussed. I further use my life design time to think on and evaluate my progress. Your life design time is your thinking time. John Maxwell, who has an entire book on thinking for success says, "thinking precedes achievement." I also use this time to express gratitude for that which has already been accomplished and for that which I expect to be accomplished.

LESSON 96: DESIGNING THE WEEK AND DAYS IN ADVANCE

Jim Rohn is my favourite personal development coach and he has said some unforgettable things.

Concerning the design of the day, here is what he said that has stayed with me, "Either you run the day or it will run you... You should see your day before it begins. See your week before it begins." One of the habits of successful people is learning to set priorities and practising good time management. A good way to do this is to list all the activities that you need to do at the start of the week. This includes for me time with family and friends, time for rest and time for work. I usually give myself one unplugged day to relax, rest and recharge each week. I try not to use social media on these days, reduce phone calls and if possible, not to turn on my computer. After listing all the activities, I look at the deadlines for each and then choose the most important ones to be completed each day. Then I plan ahead for each day by making a list of five things to do the night or evening before the next day. In this way, I end up planning my week and days ahead of time.

Sometimes I write down things to achieve for every 100 days and then break the list up into months and then weeks. When all the things to do seem overwhelming, I concentrate on the most important thing to be done each day or the activity to be done at a particular point in the day and nothing more. If I achieve only one thing each day and it is the most important, then that day is a success. Planning each day in advance and putting it in writing helps me to sleep better. I don't have to worry about what to do the next day. I don't have to rely on memory. It reduces my levels of anxiety and helps me to live in 24 hour compartments which again, greatly reduces my worry habit and anxiety levels.

Choosing 1-5 activities in order of importance helps me to make valuable use of my time. It also gives me room for eventualities and unexpected occurrences. When I put these things on paper, when those emergencies are taken care of, I know how to regain focus. Each week I review the list and see what unfinished tasks need to be carried over to the next week or left alone. The habit of designing my week and planning the day in advance has been one of the most rewarding habits that I have adopted. It helps me run the day so it does not run me.

LESSON 97: NOURISHING THE MIND

Each day I listen to uplifting and educational material to build my faith and increase my knowledge, skills and attitudes. I love listening to stories of success and teachings on success. I practise listening to audio books while I work at home and when I commute. I listen to messages recorded on my phone during wait periods and in between appointments. To become more, we have to learn more and to earn more, we have to learn more. My friend Vincent Walker once told me that what you know will put you on a ledge. I also believe the more you know, the greater your edge.

LESSON 98: RISING EARLY

I find rising early to be extremely beneficial to me. This is the time I have control over my day and almost no distraction. I find that not checking emails or using social media in the first hour or two of my day leads to greater productivity. I have also noted that men and women of significance and many high achievers throughout history have been early risers. I am usually up by 4:30 each morning. Six o'clock rarely catches me in my bed even on weekends. I would rather get up early and prepare for the day and return to sleep than to let 6 o'clock catch me in bed. Brian Tracy lists this as one of the main habits of successful people. Rising early is the golden hour and a great time to review your goals, pray, exercise, read and set the tone for the day. I find in this regard, the proverb, brought into common usage by Benjamin Franklyn, true to form, "early to bed, early to rise, makes a man wealthy, healthy and wise."

LESSON 99: MAKING TIME TO SERVE AND CONTRIBUTE

Work is not a sin. Each week we should set aside time to contribute to make our family, community and society better. Making a contribution is part of fulfilling purpose. Have you ever wondered why the average age of survival after retirement is three years? Work is essential to our survival. We should see our jobs in this light and not just something that pays the bills. It was Zig Ziglar who wisely said, if you help enough people get what they want, you will eventually get what you want. Jim Rohn says, success is in the service of others, not at the expense of others. Jesus, the Master teacher, taught that the greatest among us is the one who serves. We are also paid by the quality and quantity of our service or the value of our service.

There is also great value in serving without expecting material rewards. If you can schedule giving back time in your week, it would be great. Doing something special for an elderly person, for your neighbour or a service organization, for the poor, marginalized, disabled, homeless or hungry. Taking time to help others achieve their goals is one of the highest forms of service. Success is fulfilling our life assignment which invariable means making a contribution, doing something of worth, while living on earth.

LESSON 100: CONNECTING WITH FAMILY AND FRIENDS

Have you ever wondered why solitary confinement is a punishment and perhaps the greatest of all punishment in prison? I believe it is because we are wired for relationships without which life has no zest or real meaning and without which we die a slow painful death. No man is an island. We cannot be successful by ourselves. It is no fun being alone. We should make sure that each week we connect with the people who matter most to us. For me these times of connection include attending church, a phone call to a friend or family member, eating Sunday dinners with my family whenever I can, praying with a friend or just calling to check up and letting them know how much I appreciate them. When you have as many friends as I do, sometimes it is a challenge to keep up but I am so happy for those whose friendships are like blood connections. It is not the frequency of connection that makes the connection meaningful.

Connecting intentionally should be our priority. We should not wait for illness or disaster to connect. Maintaining these connections will pay off in tragedy and crisis. I know it has for me and it makes my life so much more rewarding and is a habit of success that we should all adopt. What is the point of work and achieving all these goals if we end up unhappy, friendless and alone? Remember, "if you want to go fast, go alone but if you want to go far, go together." At the end of it all, I believe true success at its core is in maintaining a happy and healthy relationship with our Creator and with each other or the people who matter most to us. It is a life based on serving and loving God and loving people as we love ourselves.

IT'S TIME TO DEVELOP YOUR SUCCESS HABITS

As you reflect on my habits of success, will you adopt them? It's time to develop habits that will lead to your success. Study the habits of successful people and see which ones are right for you and then adopt them. Once you do, your life will change and you will indeed live a meaningful, productive and successful life.

RESPONSE TO TREE TALK

What actions will you take as a result of this tree talk? Or what decisions will you make?

A FINAL WORD

Congratulations on completing this 31 day journey! I don't know where you were on your journey when you started reading this book or where you are now. Perhaps you are facing financial struggles like I did in pursuing my dream. Perhaps you are at a point of transition and are now filled with clarity and hope for the future. I don't know what decisions you have made as a result of these lessons but wherever you are, I believe this final word will further challenge you and prove beneficial on your success journey.

Does the farmer worry about what's happening to the seed while it is in the soil? No! That's none of his business! He has faith and confidence that once there is rain and sunshine and he does his part to fertilize it, that growth will take place. The farmer does not frustrate himself trying to figure out what's happening to the seed while it is in the soil. That's foolish and a waste of time! He sees the end, that is, the vision of the harvest, he does his part, waits for it and makes a plan for the harvest.

Therefore, do not frustrate yourself trying to figure out all the details of how and when your dream will manifest. Do your part and exercise patience and hope like the farmer because whether it is the great oak tree, the magnificent palm tree, the colourful maple tree or a small tree, none of these attained their full height overnight. This is a lesson that I have repeated throughout this book and it is significant. Remember the trees when you get discouraged while pursuing that all important goal of yours, be it marriage, education, financial independence, career or making a difference in the world. Personal growth and development is progressive. Success is the gradual achievement of your vision, worthy ideal or goal. Be patient. Believe that one day like the trees you will reach your full height.

I also want to further challenge you in the meantime. If your life is spared, five or ten years from now, you will arrive at some destination. The question is: where? Will it be a well designed one or an un-designed destination? Success is not by accident, it is intentional. And what if you apply the principles and lessons taught in this book? I know that if you do, your rewards will be phenomenal. Therefore, apply the principles and feed the dream even when it seems like you are not making progress and doubts arise as you face obstacles and delays. Remember, God, your Divine Designer, has created you with inbuilt mechanisms, gifts and abilities to fulfill that destiny. Trust your Divine Designer to release the resources and the relationships to bring your vision to pass.

You are designed to win. You are in the process of becoming and you're on your way. Remember the Chinese bamboo tree. Development is taking place. You will grow 90 feet tall! Your vision is possible. Keep watering and fertilizing it and don't give up! YOU can live the meaningful, productive and successful life you were designed to live. Remember, talk, grow and live successfully like the trees!

GRATEFUL ACKNOWLEDGEMENTS

I am grateful to my Life Designer and Heavenly Father who continues to inspire me and encourage me through his creation to live with purpose and to continue my journey on the path less travelled. This book owes a debt of gratitude to the following:

To my landlady, Mrs. Barbara Harrison, who planted the trees in our backyard which have given me such wonderful insights on life and success, thank you for providing such wonderful inspiration!

To Jim Rohn (Mr. Self Development), Brian Tracy, John Maxwell, Earl Nightingale and Les Brown, your thoughts and writings are major signposts on my journey of personal development.

To my mom, Mavarene Davy-Gordon, my siblings Najwa and Noel and my sister-in-law, Natisha, I am supremely grateful for your support along the journey. Your support has meant the world to me.

To Rev. Herro Blair Jnr., your prophetic insights, guidance and support enabled me to complete yet another book. You are right, "I will grow old writing to transform lives. The books in me will not die but will be used for greater impact."

To my friend, Didan Ashanta, your work and mission serve as a source of inspiration and your advice on writing and publishing has been invaluable. It's been a wonderful privilege to have you in my corner.

To Dr. Dameon Black, Jheanelle Foster and Kenyatta Lewis, thanks for reading through the manuscript, providing feedback and offering wonderful insights which have enhanced the content of the manuscript.

To Rev. Dr. Naila Ricketts and the Prayer 2000 family; to my EMI Team, Allanzo, Davia, Petal, Laura-Lu, Damion, Tamara, Camece, Paulette, Jeweleen, Denesha, Stephanie, Sheril and Vonorica for your support and encouragement along the journey

To the Butterly 276 Group, for your wise and timely advice and support at a critical juncture in the publishing process.

To all my endorsers and followers on social media, for reading my blogs and sharing your thoughts on these tree talks. Your feedback inspired the publication.

To my publishing team, whose wisdom and expertise polished and transformed mere words into a beautiful and very desirable package.

To Mr. Richard Scholefield, of Phoenix Printery, whose kindness and guidance made printing locally much easier than I had anticipated. I'm forever grateful.

NOTES

PART I:
TALK LIKE TREES

TALK 5

1. Richard Branson. Web. July 23, 2013.
   http://www.virgin.com/entrepreneur/richard-branson-failure.
2. Jack Canfield, Mark Victor Hansen, Amy Newmark. Chicken Soup for the Soul 20th Anniversary Edition: All Your Favourite Original Stories Plus 20 Bonus Stories for the Next 20 Years Web. February 23, 2015. http//www.amazon.com.
3. Chicken Soup for the Soul. *Facts and Figures*. Web. October 19, 2015.
   http://www.chickensoup.com/about/facts-and-figures
4. Dr. Mary Lu Arpaia and Dr. Ben Faber. Avocado Information. November 8, 2015. Web.
   http://ucavo.ucr.edu/General/Answers.html#anchor1425683

TALK 7

5. *Moringa Medicine, Health Benefits*. Web. July 18, 2015.
   miracletrees.org/moringa_medicine.html

Talk 8

6. *Meaning of the Colour Green*. Web. January 25, 2011. www.bourncreative.com/meaning-of-the-color-green/

Talk 9

7. Tropical Permaculture. *How to Grow Banana Plants and Keep Them Happy.* Web. November 11, 2015. http://www.tropicalpermaculture.com/growing-bananas.html.

PART II:
Grow Like Trees

Talk 14

8. *The Different Types of Trees.* Web. November 2015. http://typeslist.com/different-types-of- trees/
9. Nick Vujijic. *The Incredible Love Story of Nick Vujicic and His Wife.* Web. June 7, 2013. https://www.youtube.com/watch?v=s3QezBvN1BE.

Talk 17

10. Skoll Archives Foundation. *Social Entrepreneurship.* Web. September 22, 2015. https://skollworldforum.org/about/what-is-social-entrepreneurship/

PART III:
LIVE SUCCESSFULLY LIKE TREES

TALK 21

11. Mail Online. *The Suicide Map of the Year.* Web. November 11, 2015. http://www.dailymail.co.uk/news/article-2743457/WHO-calls-action-reduce-global-suicide-rate-800-000-year.html
12. Myles Munroe. Quotes. https://www.thecable.ng/wealthiest-place-earth-cemetery-%E2%94%80-memorable-munroe-quotes

TALK 22

13. Save a Tree. Web. November 2015. http://www.savatree.com/whytrees.html#sthash.3UyI7HOm.dpuf

TALK 23

14. Mary Theresa. 2001. *Healing for Bruised Souls: A Church Training Manual.* Pittsburg: GOALS Ministries.
15. Brian Tracy. 2013. *Time Management.* American Management Association. Web. www.amanet.org

TALK 24

16. Brian Tracy. 2013. *Time Management.* American Management Association. Web. www.amanet.org
17. Earl Nightingale. *The $25,000 Idea.* Web. November 8, 2015. http://www.nightingale.com/articles/the-25000-idea/

TALK 27

18. Working Resources. *The Art of the Goal.* Web. November 2015. http://www.workingresources.com/professionaleffectivenessarticles/the-art-of-the-goal.html
19. John Rampton. *9 Success Habits of Wealthy People That Cost Nothing.* Web. November 8, 2015. http://www.entrepreneur.com/article/249269

TALK 28

20. Character Training Blog. What is Character? Web. November 8, 2015. http://www.character-training.com/blog/

TALK 30

21. Jim Rohn. Web. December 17, 2015. http://www.mrselfdevelopment.com/2010/02/7-life-lessons-from-jim-rohn-2/

TALK 31

22. Warren Dockter. Winston Churchill's 10 most important speeches. Web. January 2015.
http://www.telegraph.co.uk/news/winston-churchill/11366880/Winston-Churchills-10-most-important-speeches.html

GET READY FOR TRANSFORMATION

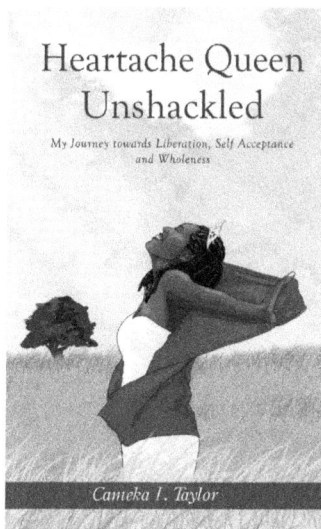

Heartache Queen
Unshackled

My Journey towards Liberation, Self Acceptance
and Wholeness

Cameka I. Taylor

Can your heartaches be healed and transformed into something beautiful? In her mentoring and teaching autobiography, *Heartache Queen Unshackled*, Cameka "Ruth" Taylor answers with a resounding YES! This book captures the story of how her experiences of years of heartache were transformed into something beautiful. It shows her pathway to liberation, healing and transformation from many years of struggle with the pain of rejection, poor self-worth and fear. Her heartaches include separation from her parents, two lung collapses, two broken engagements and many more experiences. The book makes recommendations to guide the reader to experience his/her own healing and transformation.